It Came From Mars

This is a work of fiction. All of the characters, events, and organizations portrayed in this work are either products of the authors' imagination or used fictitiously.

It Came From Mars

ISBN-13: 978-0692271698
ISBN-10: 0692271694

For information about production rights, contact:
www.jzettelmaier.com

Published by Sordelet Ink

Cover by David Blixt

IT CAME FROM MARS

A PLAY BY

JOSEPH ZETTELMAIER

Published by
Sordelet Ink

IT CAME FROM MARS received its world premiere on Feb. 18, 2010 as a co-production between The Performance Network Theatre (Ann Arbor, MI) and Williamston Theatre (Williamston, MI). It was directed by Tony Caselli. Set Design by Janine Woods-Thoma, Lighting Design by Dan Walker, Sound Design by Will Myers, Costume Design by Sally Converse-Doucette, Prop Design by Charles Sutherland. The production was stage managed by Rochelle Clark.

The cast was as follows:

QUENTIN FARLOWE: Wayne David Parker
MAUDE MYRTLES: Morgan Chard
WERNER KREILIG: Jacob Hodgson
GEORGE LOOMIS: Joseph Albright
DOLORES BRECKENRIDGE: Alysia Kolascz
JULIA CRANE: Sandra Birch

NOTE: Obtaining the production rights of this script does not include ownership of the audio materials referenced herein.

CAST OF CHARACTERS

QUENTIN FARLOWE - 40s-50s, director/writer/actor
MAUDE MYRTLES - 30s-40s, secretary
WERNER KREILIG - 20s, sound effects technician
GEORGE LOOMIS - 40s, actor, former soldier
DOLORES BRECKINRIDGE - 20s, actress
JULIA CRANE - 40s, actress

TIME
October 30, 1938

PLACE
The rehearsal room of WHQN Studios, New York

ACT I

(Lights up. MAUDE is carving a pumpkin onstage, listening to the radio. The door flies open and QUENTIN enters dramatically. He has coffee with him, clearly agitated.)

QUENTIN
Maude. We're doomed.

(QUENTIN downs the coffee.)

MAUDE
I beg your pardon?

QUENTIN
How does he expect me to do it?! That's what I'd like to know! Damn you, Jerome Albertson! Damn you straight to the very bowels of hell!

MAUDE
What did Mr. Alberts...?

QUENTIN
The man's a damned fool, that's what he is! One

rehearsal?! If he wants to bend me over, he could at least buy me dinner first! It's not enough that I'm trying to put on a quality program with a skeleton crew. Now he expects me to perform a miracle, and gives me no time to do it! What did I do to deserve this, Maude? THAT'S what I'd like to know.

MAUDE
I'm sure it's nothing pers...

QUENTIN
I was on Broadway, Maude. Did I ever tell you that?

MAUDE
You may have mentioned it, yes.

QUENTIN
It was glorious. The resources, the adoration...and now this. Left to rot in the soulless vacuum of radio, alone.

MAUDE
You're not alone, sir. You've got a fine company of...

QUENTIN
Of what? Actors? I have no actors! I have a debutante who barely qualifies as an idiot. A sound-effects man with almost no grasp on the English language.

MAUDE
What about George?

QUENTIN
Between you and me, Maude, the man has one voice and two volumes: Loud and Louder. He's as subtle as an epileptic chimpanzee. No, the only two actors in this ragtag lot are me and Agnes.

MAUDE
Oh! Mr. Farlowe! I almost forgot! Agnes...

QUENTIN
Of course! Agnes! The jewel in my crown. I tell you, if it weren't for her, I'd drive this whole company into the Hudson. If we are to pull off Mr. Albertson's miracle, it will be because of her brilliance.

MAUDE
That's lovely. But...

QUENTIN
She brings a sort of untamed sexuality to every role she plays. A smoldering intensity that forces you to hang on her every word, wouldn't you agree?

MAUDE
Oh. Um. I suppose so?

QUENTIN
Yes, she is a creature of great passion. If you get my drift. Maude.

MAUDE
I get it, sir.

QUENTIN
By god, you're right! We can do this!

MAUDE
What?

QUENTIN
With my words and Agnes' talent, we may yet prevail! Thank you, sweet Maude. Thank you.

MAUDE
But I didn't...you're welcome?

QUENTIN
My god, I want to fuck something!

(QUENTIN *notices the jack-o- lantern for the first time.*)

QUENTIN
Maude, there's a jack-o-lantern in my rehearsal space.

MAUDE
Yes, I'm sorry. I was just carving it for the children.

QUENTIN
I thought you were barren.

MAUDE
No, sir. My Dominic and I just...

QUENTIN
Fascinating. Make it go away.

(*She puts the pumpkin on her cart.*)

QUENTIN
Doesn't trick-or-treating happen tomorrow? Not on the eve of All Hallow's Eve?

MAUDE
It's a community program, sir. A lot of parents are concerned about their children running into hooligans on Halloween proper.

QUENTIN
Well, there's church-folk for you.

(MAUDE *starts setting up the space.*)

QUENTIN
Just keep those urchins out of the building.

MAUDE
I'll just greet them at the doorway.

QUENTIN
See that you do. I'll not have them interrupting my rehearsal with their trick-or-treatery.

MAUDE
I'll keep them out of your hair.

(Beat. QUENTIN runs his hands through his thinning hair.)

MAUDE
I'm so sorry.

QUENTIN
Out.

MAUDE
Mr. Farlowe, I...

QUENTIN
Out, damn you! OUT!

(She bolts. He then takes out a flask and takes a long drink. He puts it back in his jacket.)

QUENTIN
Maude. Come back.

(She does so.)

QUENTIN
I'm sorry about that. I don't mean to shout.

MAUDE
It's all right.

QUENTIN
You've the patience of a saint.

MAUDE
I don't know about all that.

QUENTIN
I'm not an easy man to work for. I know that.

MAUDE
With.

(Beat.)

MAUDE
I work with you. I work for WHQN.

QUENTIN
I am WHQN.

MAUDE
I'm not sure the board of directors would agree.
Sir.

QUENTIN
I gave this station art, I gave it legitimacy.

MAUDE
Good thing for Mr. Welles then, hmm?

(QUENTIN glares at her.)

MAUDE
I just mean...because that's where the station got
the idea for your show. From Orson Welles' Mercury
Theatre of...the umm...Air.

QUENTIN
Our work is completely different. They do trash!
Dracula, Treasure Island...

MAUDE
I like Trea....

QUENTIN
What I give people are original stories! Plucked from my own mind and painstakingly put to paper. I create, Maude. Orson Welles merely...re-creates.

MAUDE
I suppose you're right. His program's just as bad off as yours.

(Beat.)

QUENTIN
Where is Agnes? She's always early.

MAUDE
OH! Mr. Farlowe, I'm sorry. I forgot that...

QUENTIN
What? What is it?

MAUDE
Agnes phoned.

QUENTIN
Ah. Is she going to be late?

MAUDE
She just said to phone her back.

QUENTIN
And...?

MAUDE
And I'm staying out of it.

QUENTIN
You're a credit to your profession, Maude.

(He storms out, calling Agnes from the reception desk. MAUDE begins laying out the printed scripts and otherwise setting up for the rehearsal. WERNER is

heard offstage.)

WERNER
(offstage) Good evening, Mr. Farlowe.

QUENTIN
(offstage) Yes, yes. Move along.

(WERNER enters. He is a young man from Germany who serves as the company's sound effects technician. His English is good, but not perfect.)

WERNER
Hello, Miss Myrtles.

MAUDE
Oh! Hello, Werner.

WERNER
You are good on today?

MAUDE
I'm very well, thank you. And it's MRS. Myrtles, remember?

WERNER
Oh. Yes. I am sorry, I...

MAUDE
It's fine, dear.

WERNER
I will get it.

MAUDE
I know.

(He begins putting a piece of candy on everyone's scripts.)

MAUDE
What's that you're doing?

WERNER
Candy.

MAUDE
I can see that.

WERNER
For Halloween, yes?

(He gives her a piece of candy as well.)

MAUDE
You got all of us candy.

WERNER
Yes.

MAUDE
Werner! You're such a dear.

WERNER
Danke.

MAUDE
This is so thoughtful.

WERNER
My mama say tomorrow is a wicked day. That it teaches children to beg. But I like it.

MAUDE
How is your mother, dear?

WERNER
Good. She goes to see a movie tonight.

MAUDE
So she doesn't have to give out candy?

WERNER
Yes.

MAUDE
Well, don't be surprised if you have soap on your windows when you get home.

(He stares at her, confused.)

MAUDE
That's what the children do, dear. If they can't treat, they trick.

(He's still confused.)

MAUDE
Just harmless pranks. Throwing eggs at doors, rubbing soap on the windows.

WERNER
Oh.

MAUDE
Except those Bowers boys. They like to start fires.

WERNER
I should go home.

MAUDE
I'm not sure Mr. Farlowe would appreciate that.

WERNER
I must protect my house.

MAUDE
Werner, it's nothing. Really. Just children being children.

WERNER
Mama will be angry. And then she will drink.

MAUDE
I'm sure everything will be fine. It's the day before Halloween, after all. What's the worst that could

happen?

WERNER
But...

MAUDE
Besides, you don't want to leave before Dolores gets here, do you?

(WERNER smiles, becoming self-conscious.)

MAUDE
Just get your machines, dear. The others will be here soon.

(WERNER goes to the closet, and begins pulling out various sound-effect devices. He sets them on one end of the table.)

MAUDE
Ooo. What's that one?

WERNER
For making thunder.

(He shakes the thunder sheet.)

MAUDE
Oh, that's just wonderful.

WERNER
This is my favorite.

(He pulls out a wind machine and cranks it. MAUDE is clearly impressed.)

MAUDE
My goodness.

WERNER
I listened to Frankenstein on Witch's Tale. My

friend say this is how they make the wind, so I build myself.

MAUDE
Aren't you clever?

WERNER
It is not so difficult. You wrap the cloth around the...

MAUDE
You used it in The Monster of Dr. Monstroso.

WERNER
Yes! For the storm, when the Doctor brings his metal man to life.

(WERNER gets excited, and begins acting out the scene. When he speaks the lines, his accent almost entirely disappears.)

WERNER
"Let the gods tremble in fear this night, for I have stolen from them their secrets. I have improved upon their designs, for where they crafted with soft and fragile flesh, I have made a man...OF STEEL!"

(MAUDE claps.)

MAUDE
Werner! That was wonderful!

(WERNER smiles and bows.)

MAUDE
You should audition for Mr. Farlowe. He'd hire you on the spot.

WERNER
I am no actor. I make noises.

MAUDE
If you say so. Oh! I saw this in the weekend paper.
The Invisible Ray is playing at that little theatre
down on Fourth.

(He goes about resetting his machines.)

WERNER
I do not know that one.

MAUDE
It came out a few years ago. Boris Karloff and Bela
Lugosi discover light rays in outer space that allow
them to see into the past.

WERNER
Karloff and Lugosi? Together?

MAUDE
Oh yes.

WERNER
And there is a monster?

MAUDE
That would be telling.

*(GEORGE enters. He is in his forties, strong, a former
military man. He walks with a slight limp. He speaks as
he enters, checking his watch.)*

GEORGE
Look at that. Seven thirty on the tick, and I'm
the only actor here on time. Imagine that. Maude,
where's...

(GEORGE notices WERNER.)

GEORGE
What's the goose-stepper doing here?

MAUDE
George...

GEORGE
Honestly, Klaus...

WERNER
Werner.

GEORGE
...shouldn't you be out massacring women and children in Belgium?

MAUDE
George Loomis!

GEORGE
Relax. Klaus knows I'm just giving him a hard time. Don't you, Klaus?

WERNER
My name. Is. Werner.

(WERNER goes back to setting up equipment.)

GEORGE
See? No harm done.

(He takes his seat at the table.)

GEORGE
Oh for fuck's sake. Where is everyone else?

MAUDE
Mr. Farlowe's on the phone with Agnes.

GEORGE
Found out about that, did he?

(GEORGE has set his leg up on one of the chairs and rubs his knee.)

MAUDE
About what exactly?

GEORGE
I saw Agnes having lunch over at Ogilvy's...oh, this
must've been last Thursday. You know Ogilvy's?
They've got this beef brisket that...

MAUDE
To the point, George.

GEORGE
No, honestly. Heinrich, you ever had beef brisket?

WERNER
I know you know what my name is.

GEORGE
I had beef bourguignon in Normandy...must've
been back in '18. Ate it right off the bare back of
a French farmgirl. Ogilvy's beef brisket is the only
thing I've ever had that comes close.

MAUDE
Back to Agnes.

GEORGE
Right. I saw her having lunch.

MAUDE
At Ogilvy's.

GEORGE
Right.

MAUDE
Last Thursday.

GEORGE
Right.

(Beat.)

MAUDE
So why is Quentin on the phone with her now?

GEORGE
Why do you think? Because of Welles.

WERNER
Orson Welles?

GEORGE
No, wishing wells. Of course Orson Welles.

MAUDE
George.

(He looks back to her.)

MAUDE
Bring it all together for us, would you?

GEORGE
Who do you think Agnes was having lunch with last
Thursday at Ogilvy's?

WERNER
Orson Welles?

GEORGE
No. Wishing wells. Of course....

WERNER
We did this already.

MAUDE
Agnes was having lunch with Orson Welles?

GEORGE
Didn't I just say that?

WERNER
Not really.

GEORGE
Oh yes. Yes, yes, yes. And they were looking very cozy.

MAUDE
Lord help us.

GEORGE
Lord help her. Five on the barrelhead says that Quentin is tearing into her like the German infantry tore into those poor souls in Antwerp.

(WERNER storms out. MAUDE glares at GEORGE.)

GEORGE
What? I took three bullets to the leg. You don't see me crying to mein mater.

MAUDE
I'm not talking to you.

GEORGE
So I pick on him. I'm an ass. I admit it. I'm just trying to give the kid a thick skin. There's worse than me out there, and you know it.

MAUDE
That's debatable at best.

GEORGE
You're not fooling anyone, you know.

MAUDE
Hmmm?

GEORGE
All that hostility towards me. The fancy airs.

Everyone knows.

(MAUDE stares at him, uncertain if she should ask.)

MAUDE
Against my better judgment, I'm going to ask what exactly you mean.

GEORGE
It's just you and me, lamb. You can admit it.

MAUDE
Oh dear god...

GEORGE
You're not the first to fall under old George's spell.

(She looks slightly ill.)

GEORGE
After all, you know what they say about actors.

MAUDE
They killed Lincoln?

GEORGE
Don't try to deny it. There's a heat between us, and you know it.

MAUDE
George.

GEORGE
Yes?

MAUDE
It would be difficult for you to be more wrong than you are this very second.

(He closes in on her.)

GEORGE
Oh, I think I could find a way.

MAUDE
Stop it.

(He smacks her bottom.)

GEORGE
All right then. Just having some fun. *(He notices the candy on his script.)* Well, well, well. What's all this then? *(He picks it up, showing it to her.)*

MAUDE
They call it candy.

GEORGE
Sweets for your sweet, hmmm?

MAUDE
It's not from me.

GEORGE
How's that?

MAUDE
It's from Werner. You know, the nice German boy you've been demoralizing all night.

GEORGE
Demoralizing? How does a sweet little thing like you learn a big old word like that?

(Finally, MAUDE closes in on him.)

MAUDE
Listen to me, you deplorable skunk of a man. I've been privately tutored since I was five years old. I attended Vassar, I speak three languages, and I wouldn't even be in this pitiful job if my father...

a drunken military man very much like yourself, I might add...hadn't put our family's money in beet farms. That's just something for you to think about while my husband pounds you into the ground like a tent post. Are we clear?

(Beat.)

GEORGE
Having our monthlies then, are we?

(MAUDE comes at him, and he bolts out of the rooming, laughing. DOLORES enters as he does, nearly getting run over.)

DOLORES
Oh my!

GEORGE
One side, Wiggles!

(He's out. DOLORES is a pretty young woman, fashionable and, to all appearances, a little vapid. She just stares at MAUDE.)

DOLORES
Did he just call me "Wiggles?"

MAUDE
I believe so.

DOLORES
Why?

MAUDE
Why does that man do anything?

(Beat.)

DOLORES
Inbreeding?

MAUDE
Rhetorical question, dear.

(DOLORES just stares at her.)

MAUDE
It means I wasn't expecting an answer.

DOLORES
Then why did you ask? *(notices the candy.)* Oooooooo! Candy! *(She takes it off her script, eating it.)* Mmmmmmm. Chocolate. Maude, you're so thoughtful.

MAUDE
Thanks. It wasn't me.

DOLORES
Beg pardon?

MAUDE
It was from Werner.

DOLORES
Werner got me candy?

MAUDE
He got everyone candy, dear.

DOLORES
Oh. How is your husband's leg?

MAUDE
Better, thank you. Dr. Haverstock thinks he'll be back on his feet soon.

DOLORES
When I was seven, my horse Duchess broke her leg. Daddy said he took her to a special farm, but I think they shot her.

(She takes a look at the script.)

DOLORES
Have you read it?

MAUDE
No.

DOLORES
I don't know how you do it. If I had to do your job,
I'd be so bored I'd read anything I could get my
hands on. But I guess that's why you do what you
do, and I do what I do.

(Beat.)

DOLORES
What is it you do, exactly?

MAUDE
I'm a receptionist.

DOLORES
My daddy has a receptionist. She's colored. I hope
we don't go too long tonight. I've got the most
wonderful party to go to. Do you know Chester
Wolcott?

MAUDE
Can't say that I...

DOLORES
He's in oil. Texas oil. I met him at the Hartford
ball. He's so big and...Texan. Anyway, he's having
the most wonderful party. A masquerade. Couldn't
you die?

MAUDE
I really, really could.

DOLORES
So if you could tell Quentin to keep it snappy, that would be lovely.

MAUDE
Quentin...Mr. Farlowe doesn't listen to me.

DOLORES
Oh, he doesn't listen to anyone. He just goes on and on and on. Don't you just hate people who go on and on and on?

MAUDE
As a matter...

DOLORES
There's no getting a word in edgewise with that man. He starts going on about his theatrical career... that show he wrote...

MAUDE
The Stain Upon My Soul.

DOLORES
You'd think he was the toast of Broadway, the way he talks. I'd almost call him erudite if he wasn't so myopic.

(Beat.)

DOLORES
Where is Quentin? Chop-chop and all that.

(WERNER enters.)

DOLORES
Hello, Werner.

WERNER
Hello, Ms. Breckinridge.

DOLORES
Werner, you can call me Dolores.

WERNER
Dolores.

DOLORES
"Ms. Breckinridge." He's so proper. Couldn't you die?

WERNER
Someone is dying?

MAUDE
It's an expression, dear. How's Mr. Farlowe doing?

WERNER
He is red-colored. And yelling.

DOLORES
Why?

MAUDE
Agnes was meeting with Orson Welles.

DOLORES
Ooooooooooh. I bet he didn't like that. Quentin, I mean. Not Orson.

MAUDE
Safe bet.

WERNER
You look very pretty.

DOLORES
Why, thank you. I've been invited to a party tonight.

WERNER
Oh.

DOLORES
That's assuming we get out of here at a reasonable hour. Who holds rehearsals on Halloween, anyway?

MAUDE
Halloween's tomorrow, dear.

DOLORES
Either way. It's unpatriotic.

(GEORGE re-enters.)

GEORGE
Well, they can only afford one rehearsal. Let's take what we can get, eh?

DOLORES
Hello, George.

GEORGE
Wiggles.

WERNER
What do you mean?

GEORGE
Hmmm?

MAUDE
They can only afford one rehearsal, so we should take what we can get?

GEORGE
When I said "we", I was referring to the talent, Maude.

MAUDE
George, what are you talking about?

GEORGE
Did you notice that there's no broadcast tonight?

Any thoughts as to why, little Miss Vassar?

WERNER
We have no money?

GEORGE
Yavohl. WHQN lost three sponsors this week,
including Listerine.

MAUDE
But...but Listerine was our biggest sponsor! We've
been running their commercials for years.

GEORGE
I know! It cleared my dandruff right up. But now...

MAUDE
Oh dear.

DOLORES
We have no money?

GEORGE
And the last horse crosses the finish line.

WERNER
But...I need this job!

DOLORES
So do I!

GEORGE
Please. You can just dip into daddy's trust fund. But
what about an old warhorse like me? Or a spinster
like Maude?

MAUDE
Spinsters aren't married, you idiot.

GEORGE
And what about poor Wolfgang here? He's lucky

enough to land a job with Quentin, but most employers...they're not exactly eager to hire krauts, hmm?

WERNER
I am a hard worker! I do good work!

DOLORES
No one's denying that. George, stop panicking everyone.

GEORGE
I'm just telling you what I heard.

MAUDE
From whom?

GEORGE
Quentin. It's amazing what happens when you talk to someone rather than about them.

MAUDE
Don't you high-horse with me. You're the biggest gossip in eight city blocks.

GEORGE
What about those old Irish biddies next door?

(Beat.)

MAUDE
Neck-and-neck.

DOLORES
Maybe I can ask daddy to donate again.

GEORGE
Quentin already tried. The old skinflint drew up his purse strings like that.

(GEORGE snaps.)

DOLORES
Don't call my daddy a skinflint.

GEORGE
I wouldn't if he didn't give me such a damn good reason.

WERNER
Mr. Breckenridge already give us money last month.

GEORGE
Yes, yes. Times is hard all over.

MAUDE
We can't...I need this job...we have a mortgage. Dominic's laid out for another two weeks...

GEORGE
What's the matter this time?

DOLORES
Broken leg.

MAUDE
Oh god. We need my paychecks.

*(In a fit of frustration, WERNER takes a small maga-
zine out of his pocket and throws it across the room.)*

DOLORES
Oh my!

WERNER
Why!? Why did I buy this? I am indulgent. I think
I have a good job, but...

MAUDE
Calm down, dear.

(DOLORES has retrieved the magazine.)

DOLORES
Astounding Science Fiction. I didn't know you read this.

MAUDE
He loves space stories. He's a very imaginative boy, aren't you, Werner?

WERNER
Twenty-five cents! That is what I paid, and now it is gone! What will I tell mama?

(DOLORES *has begun flipping through the magazine.* GEORGE *looks over her shoulder.*)

GEORGE
Treasure Asteroid? Are you serious?

DOLORES
Hush. This is a good issue.

GEORGE
You read that trash?

WERNER
Not trash!

DOLORES
Daddy has a subscription. I flip through it now and then.

WERNER
I am at Gimbel's and I see it on the rack. A new story by D.B. Pennyworth. So I think "Is alright, Werner. You have worked hard. Go ahead and buy the magazine."

MAUDE
Pennyworth's his favorite.

DOLORES
Really?

WERNER
My poor mama. I have failed her.

(The door swings open. QUENTIN enters, a ball of barely-contained rage.)

QUENTIN
Maude, to me.

(MAUDE goes to him.)

QUENTIN
I need you to go to Weybridge Apartments. You know where that is?

MAUDE
Two blocks south.

QUENTIN
I need you to get Julia.

GEORGE
Good god, man!

QUENTIN
Tell her I need her.

MAUDE
Are you sure about this?

(GEORGE grabs QUENTIN's shoulders.)

GEORGE
Think about what you're doing. I'm begging you.

QUENTIN
I don't have any other goddamn options.

MAUDE
But why send me?

QUENTIN
Because if I ask her, she'll say no. But she likes you.
Beg. Plead if you have to. Explain to her that it's a
part only she can play. Appeal to her ego.

GEORGE
Lord knows she's got enough of it.

QUENTIN
Promise her anything. Anything but money. But get
her over here. Immediately.

MAUDE
I...alright.

QUENTIN
Now go. Go, go, go.

(She hurries off. GEORGE calls after her.)

GEORGE
Run like your job depends on it!

(QUENTIN glares at GEORGE.)

GEORGE
Oh. Right. I told them they might be losing their
jobs.

QUENTIN
Why...would you do that?

GEORGE
Hmm. That's an excellent question.

DOLORES
Is it true? Is the station going to close?

QUENTIN
No, no, no. The station's not going to close.

(Beat.)

QUENTIN
But they may cut loose our program.

WERNER
What?!

QUENTIN
It's a possibility. That's why we have to rehearse on the sly.

WERNER
"On the...?"

GEORGE
It means WHQN doesn't know we're here.

QUENTIN
I can't afford to rent their rehearsal space.

DOLORES
But...but...

QUENTIN
Don't worry.

QUENTIN
No one's going to be here but Maude. She was kind enough to let us rehearse while she tends to the trick-or-treating. Bless her soul, she never asks questions. Oh! Dammit!

(He pulls some bills from his pockets and heads towards the door.)

DOLORES
Quentin, where are...

QUENTIN
Maude! Wait!

(He runs off after her.)

GEORGE
Five on the barrelhead says he making her pick up scotch.

WERNER
And so it has come to this.

DOLORES
All because of Agnes.

GEORGE
Not all because of Agnes.

DOLORES
The drinking is because of Agnes.

GEORGE
Fair enough.

DOLORES
I for one never knew what Quentin saw in her.

(Beat. Both GEORGE & WERNER laugh at that.)

DOLORES
What?

GEORGE
Come on. Even you aren't that dim.

DOLORES
I'm not dim!

WERNER
He means that... well, Agnes is... and she has large...

GEORGE
They were going at it like Italian sailors on shore leave.

(Beat. DOLORES just stares at them.)

GEORGE
Oh for Christ's...when a man and a woman love each other very much...

DOLORES
I understood the reference, George.

GEORGE
You sure? Because it was pretty clever.

(DOLORES goes to the door, looking for QUENTIN.)

DOLORES
I swear, Quentin only got into directing to get the attention of women who wouldn't normally give him the time of day.

GEORGE
Well! Wiggles has an opinion! Or is it something you just picked up from Daddy?

WERNER
Do not talk to her that way.

GEORGE
Now, now, children. We have to present a united front when Julia arrives.

DOLORES
George.

GEORGE
Hmmm?

DOLORES
Who is Julia?

(QUENTIN returns.)

QUENTIN
Julia Crane. My ex-wife.

DOLORES
You were married?

QUENTIN
I was on Broadway once, too. But no one wants to talk about that.

DOLORES
You talk about it.

(Beat. QUENTIN stares at her.)

DOLORES
All the time.

(Beat.)

QUENTIN
All I will say about Ms. Crane is this. She is a fine actress, who will...with some cajoling...take over Agnes' part.

WERNER
You were married?

QUENTIN
Yes, dammit! Do we have to trample the subject into the ground?

GEORGE
Steady, Quentin.

WERNER
I am sorry! I ask only because...

QUENTIN
Fifteen years! Fifteen years we were together, and I
caught her shtuping another man!

(QUENTIN grabs WERNER.)

QUENTIN
Are you happy now, Werner!? You've dragged it out
of me!

WERNER
I just...

QUENTIN
What?

WERNER
I was just...

QUENTIN
What, damn you!? Out with it!

WERNER
...I just wanted to know if she liked chocolate.

(QUENTIN releases him.)

QUENTIN
What?

DOLORES
Werner got us all chocolate. He's trying to be
nice.

QUENTIN
Oh. I see. I...my apologies, Werner. I have no idea
what came over me.

GEORGE
Oh, I have an idea.

QUENTIN
Quiet, George.

GEORGE
That hussy always brought out the worst in you.
Even when she wasn't in the room.

QUENTIN
I know. Of course I know. But what choice do I
have? Welles has fucked his way through just about
every other actress in this city.

WERNER
Not Dolores!

DOLORES
Darn right not me. Not to say he didn't try.

(They all turn and stare at her.)

DOLORES
What?

GEORGE
Orson Welles tried to bed you?

DOLORES
Well, maybe not all that. He did ask me out to
dinner...oh, about a year ago.

QUENTIN
WHAT?!

WERNER
You...went to dinner? With Orson Welles?

DOLORES
Oh, it was nothing. He tried to get me drunk.

QUENTIN
Can we stop talking about Orson Welles for two fucking minutes?!

(Beat.)

QUENTIN
We have a rehearsal to prepare for. Werner, set up your machines.

(WERNER looks around. All his machines are already out. Beat.)

WERNER
All right.

QUENTIN
Dolores, could you put a pot of coffee on? It's going to be a long night.

DOLORES
All right.

(Beat. She stops, having no idea how to make a pot of coffee. QUENTIN catches on.)

QUENTIN
Werner, go show Dolores how to make a pot of coffee.

WERNER
All right.

(He exits. QUENTIN sits, holding his stomach.)

GEORGE
Ulcer acting up?

QUENTIN
What do you think?

GEORGE
I think your ulcer's acting up.

QUENTIN
You're smarter than you look.

(Both men smirk at the joke, a ribbing between friends.)

GEORGE
You're going to be all right.

(QUENTIN stares at him, unsure what he means.)

GEORGE
You survived Julia Crane for 15 years. You can survive her for one rehearsal.

QUENTIN
Let's hope so.

GEORGE
Remember. You're the director. She's working for you. You don't have to take any of her bunk.

QUENTIN
She's bailing us out at in our moment of desperation. And she knows it.

GEORGE
Don't worry. She starts to lip off, I'll give her some of this.

(GEORGE shadow-boxes. QUENTIN smiles sadly. GEORGE catches on.)

GEORGE
It's not Julia, is it? It's Welles.

QUENTIN
It's both, I think. Just hearing his name...

GEORGE
Look at it this way. Could Welles have written The
Stain Upon My Soul? Not in his wildest dreams.
That play redefined theatre! You've told me so lots
of times.

(Beat.)

QUENTIN
That's what I like about you, George. Loyalty.

GEORGE
Nothing more important in the world.

QUENTIN
I...I'm sorry that I ever chose him over you.

GEORGE
Water under the bridge.

QUENTIN
George, I...

GEORGE
He was your protégé. I understood that.

QUENTIN
It wasn't enough that he turned his back on me. He
took everything I'd work so hard to build, everyone
who...

GEORGE
Not everyone.

*(Beat. GEORGE can tell who QUENTIN's really
thinking about.)*

GEORGE
Quentin, you've only made two mistakes in your
entire life. One was trusting Welles. The other was

marrying that loud-mouthed cellar smeller.

(QUENTIN laughs a little at that. GEORGE laughs as well.)

GEORGE
Remember when you took her flask before opening night? I walked into my dressing room, and she was trying to drink my benzene!

(They both laugh louder.)

GEORGE
You have absolutely nothing to fear from her, old top.

QUENTIN
You know what? By god, you're right.

GEORGE
Almost always.

QUENTIN
Who the hell is she? No one! Some washed-up actress living in some third-rate apartments!

GEORGE
Yes!

QUENTIN
And who am I? I'm Quentin Melville Farlowe! I'm the goddamn writer and director of the finest radio theatre in this proud country!

GEORGE
Yes!

QUENTIN
Let the rapacious harpy rain down her foulness upon me! I'll shake it off like...like...help me, George.

GEORGE
Like...um...like a cherry cordial shaking off its wrapper.

QUENTIN
Like a cherry cordial shaking off...WHAT?!

(QUENTIN stares at GEORGE)

GEORGE
I was looking at the candy.

(WERNER & DOLORES return.)

DOLORES
The coffee's on. I feel so...domestic.

WERNER
She did well. No burns.

DOLORES
Not with my Teutonic knight watching over me.

WERNER
I'm not... I was just...

QUENTIN
All right, all right. Let's try to put on a professional face, shall we?

(QUENTIN motions to their seats. They all sit down, going to their scripts. WERNER preps his machines.)

GEORGE
So what's the story this time, old top?

(DOLORES reads the title.)

DOLORES
The House That...Hell Built? Oh please.

QUENTIN
You have a problem with the title, missy?

DOLORES
Well, come now, Quentin. That Hell Built? What does that even mean?

QUENTIN
It means the house was built by a coven of Devil-worshiping witches in Colonial times.

DOLORES
Another ghost story?

(WERNER rolls some thunder. GEORGE flips through the script, underlining his lines.)

QUENTIN
Thank you, Werner. Yes, it's a ghost story. People love ghost stories.

GEORGE
....bullshit... bullshit... me... bullshit... me...

DOLORES
Who talks like this?

QUENTIN
What? What was that?

GEORGE
...bullshit... bullshit... what's that word...

DOLORES
Nothing. Nothing at all.

GEORGE
...Egom... egonimom...

QUENTIN
Do you think you could do better?

DOLORES
Well, if you're open to some constructive...

QUENTIN
Dolores, let's make one thing perfectly clear, shall we? I am the director here. I am the writer. And you are here because you can read lines with something resembling emotion without tripping over your words. Understand?

(Beat. DOLORES is cowed.)

DOLORES
I'm very sorry.

GEORGE
Egomaniacal!

(They all stare at GEORGE, who is very pleased with himself for figuring out the word.)

GEORGE
It's egomaniacal.

QUENTIN
All right. It's the standard breakdown. Dolores, you're playing Lily, and I'm playing John. Newlyweds on their way to the coast for their honeymoon. George, you'll be playing...

GEORGE
Mr. Krenshaw, the mysterious man at the gas station.

QUENTIN
Yes. You'll also be playing Inspector VanHorn, the policeman who finds their bodies at the end. Werner?

WERNER
Ja?

QUENTIN
I'm going to need creaking doors and floorboards, wind, chains and...

(WERNER *shakes the thundersheet again.*)

QUENTIN
Exactly. The story is a classic, but compelling none-theless. John and Lily are...

DOLORES
Newlyweds on their way to the coast for their honeymoon.

QUENTIN
And they stop off at this little, run-down gas station. In the middle of a thunderstorm.

(GEORGE *reads the script.*)

GEORGE
Mm-hmmm.

QUENTIN
Mr. Krenshaw warns them about the old house up the road...

GEORGE
Oh! This is golden.

(GEORGE *reads aloud, with a character voice.*)

GEORGE
"They say no one lives there now...except evil. And evil always sets the table for guests."

QUENTIN
Very nice reading. Now the couple get a flat tire...

DOLORES
On their way to the coast for their honeymoon.

QUENTIN
And will find their only sanctuary from the storm
is in...The House that Hell Built!

*(No one responds to his moment. QUENTIN glares
at WERNER. He rolls the thunder again. JULIA has
entered, and stands in the doorway. She is very confi-
dent, knowing that she is in control. MAUDE is with
her.)*

JULIA
And people say theatre's a dying art.

QUENTIN
Julia.

JULIA
Quentin.

QUENTIN
You're looking well.

JULIA
I am, aren't I?

QUENTIN
May I assume that Maude has explained our situation?

MAUDE
I...

JULIA
She told me that you need me to pull your prover-
bial fat out of the fire. I was feeling nostalgic, so
here I am.

MAUDE
Here's your...um...package.

*(She hands QUENTIN a bag w/ a bottle in it. The
sound of knocking and trick-or-treaters at the door.)*

MAUDE
Mr. Farlowe. If you... can I just...

QUENTIN
Yes, yes. Tend to the rabble.

(She heads out. An awkward moment.)

QUENTIN
Julia, this is Dolores Breckenridge, our ingénue.

DOLORES
It's a pleasure.

JULIA
Of course it is.

QUENTIN
Werner Kreilig, our sound effects man.

(WERNER offers her a chocolate.)

JULIA
A cherry cordial? Aren't you sweet. And strapping.

QUENTIN
And, of course, you remember George.

JULIA
Yes, yes. How's the leg, George?

GEORGE
Just fine. How's the great empty hole where your heart should be?

JULIA
It grows at the mere sight of you.

QUENTIN
And now that we're all acquainted, let's get started, shall we?

JULIA
Just a moment, Ducky.

QUENTIN
We're a bit pressed for time, Julia...

DOLORES
I have a party to get to.

(Beat.)

QUENTIN
So if you'll just take a seat...

JULIA
I'm not taking anything.

QUENTIN
Beg pardon?

JULIA
Maude asked me to come. I've come.

QUENTIN
Yes, and that's lovely. Let's...

JULIA
But I haven't agreed to anything.

(Beat. He just stares at her.)

JULIA
Oh, come now. After everything that's gone on between us, do you really think I'd come running back like some schoolgirl? You broke my heart.

QUENTIN
You slept with...

JULIA
Be that as it may. I've not even heard a peep from

you in over a year now. But suddenly, you come calling at my door.

GEORGE
Well, Maude came calling.

JULIA
Let the grown-ups talk, George.

QUENTIN
All right, all right. What is it you want? If it's money, you've made the trip for nothing. I can't offer more than scale. But...

JULIA
Oh, I think you know what I want.

QUENTIN
No. I don't.

JULIA
Yes. You do.

QUENTIN
Haven't the foggiest.

JULIA
Don't make me spell it out to you.

QUENTIN
Just tell me. The clock is ticking.

JULIA
I remember you being more fun than this. What I want, my dear Quentin, is for you...to beg.

(Beat.)

QUENTIN
You must be joking.

JULIA
Oh, must I?

GEORGE
Don't do it, man. We can find someone else...

JULIA
At this late hour? Of my caliber? I doubt it.

DOLORES
Can we please just get going?

JULIA
Come along, sweet. Say those words that you swore you'd never say again, and I'm all yours. Of course, if your pride means that much to you, please remain silent. Perhaps this little biscuit could do the role.

DOLORES
(shocked, to WERNER) Did she just call me a biscuit?

(Long beat.)

QUENTIN
I need you, Julia.

JULIA
How badly?

QUENTIN
Oh come on!

JULIA
Have a lovely evening, all....

QUENTIN
Badly. I need you. Very badly. Please, rescue us in this, our darkest hour.

(JULIA smiles, taking it all in.)

JULIA
My god... you spend so much time imagining what
this moment will be like, and then it happens and...
delicious.

QUENTIN
All right. Let's get going.

JULIA
Like honey on my lips.

QUENTIN
Are you quite finished?

JULIA
Oh, I haven't even started. So tell me, Ducky...

QUENTIN
Don't call me that.

JULIA
What's the plan for this evening, hmm? I was ready
to settle in before Maude came begging at my door-
step.

QUENTIN
It's a meaty character roll, just like the old days.

JULIA
Mm-hmm.

QUENTIN
It requires an actress of great range and...

JULIA
What's it called?

QUENTIN
Well, the title of the piece is...

(JULIA takes a script and reads.)

JULIA
The House That...well, that's just terrible.

DOLORES
I knew it!

JULIA
And what's my part? Wealthy socialite? The mysterious but alluring foreigner?

QUENTIN
You'll be playing the witch.

GEORGE
Ha!

QUENTIN
The ghost of a witch, actually.

(She rubs her eyes.)

JULIA
I'm going to need a drink. Werner, is it?

WERNER
Ja?

JULIA
Be a dear and fetch me...

(QUENTIN sets his booze in front of her.)

JULIA
Well, what the wait staff lacks in manners, it makes up for in timing.

(She drinks, then leafs through the script.)

JULIA
So when do we go up?

QUENTIN
Sunday.

JULIA
How many rehearsals?

QUENTIN
One, including tonight.

JULIA
God. Well, at least it's one of your scripts.

(Beat.)

QUENTIN
What exactly does that mean?

JULIA
That it's short. And that it won't require a great deal of depth.

GEORGE
You don't know. You haven't even read it yet.

JULIA
Well, they're all variations on the same theme, aren't they?

QUENTIN
Don't start.

JULIA
A couple meets their untimely end at the hands of some sort of spook.

QUENTIN
You must sleep so soundly under your blanket statements.

DOLORES
Well, she's...um...

QUENTIN
Let's just rehearse, shall we?

DOLORES
I mean, I've played basically the same character for three months.

(Beat. She looks to JULIA.)

DOLORES
That's how long I've been here.

JULIA
Well, my dear, get ready for many months of the same.

GEORGE
That's enough!

WERNER
...not if we lose our jobs...

GEORGE
Oh, now look what you've started.

QUENTIN
No one's losing their... let's start on page one.

JULIA
What is he talking about?

QUENTIN
Absolutely nothing. Let's begin.

(QUENTIN reads. The others follow suit.)

QUENTIN
(as the narrator) Tonight's tale takes us on a dark road, one rarely traveled. Those who know of it avoid it, for this road does not lead to sunny shores or scenic venues. When this road ends, it simply...ends.

(DOLORES stifles a snicker. QUENTIN glares at her.)

DOLORES
I'm sorry.

QUENTIN
On this twisting road, we...

JULIA
How many times are you going to say "Road"?

QUENTIN
Excuse me?

JULIA
It's just, you've already used it... let's see... four times. And we're only a few sentences in.

QUENTIN
The story begins on a road.

DOLORES
Five times.

QUENTIN
AND the road also serves as a metaphor for...

JULIA
Here we go.

GEORGE
We are trying to rehearse here!

JULIA
Everything's a damn metaphor for you, isn't it?

GEORGE
Why don't we take it from the gas station?

(WERNER scans the script, trying to determine where they are. He starts to shake the chains as he reads.)

GEORGE
(reading Mr. Krenshaw) Well, what brings you nice folks to my old station?

DOLORES
Where are we?

GEORGE
Next page.

DOLORES
All right. Let me just...

(She finds the page.)

DOLORES
(As LILY) Well, it looks...

QUENTIN
It's my line, Dolores.

DOLORES
Sorry.

QUENTIN
(As JOHN) Well, it looks as though our tire's gotten itself a flat.

JULIA
Very original.

QUENTIN
(as JOHN) And I was wondering if you might have a spare.

GEORGE
(As KRENSHAW) Well, let me just...

QUENTIN
Werner! Enough with the damn chains!

(WERNER stops. He slowly reaches for the thunder-sheet.)

QUENTIN
No thunder either! Just sit down.

(He sits next to DOLORES, speaking to her quietly.)

WERNER
I do not know where I am.

(DOLORES shows him in the script.)

DOLORES
Right...there.

(GEORGE glares at them.)

DOLORES
Please go on.

GEORGE
(As KRENSHAW) Well, let me take a look. I think I might just have something for you lovely newlyweds.

JULIA
How does he know they're newlyweds?

GEORGE
...FOR YOU LOVELY NEWLYWEDS. Just wait here a moment.

DOLORES
(As LILY) Oh John, can't you just imagine it? Soon we'll be basking in the beauty of Shell Beach.

QUENTIN
(As JOHN) I certain hope so, Lily. But those fore-boding storm clouds give me pause.

DOLORES
(as LILY) Oh, John. Must you be so gloomy? I'm
sure they will pass long before we arrive at our
honeymoon destination.

JULIA
When do we get to my part?

(They set down their scripts.)

JULIA
I'm sorry. I just assumed that, since I was called here
in the midst of a panic, I might actually get a chance
to rehearse. Tonight.

QUENTIN
Julia, we're trying to...

GEORGE
Let me handle this, Quentin. *(To JULIA)* I know
you've been out of the game for a while, but those
of us who still work believe in following the protocol. And that protocol is to rehearse whatever the
director says. And the director is the gentleman
sitting right there who somehow found it in his
heart to bring you back into the fold. So why don't
you shut those ever-flapping lips of yours and try to
behave like a goddamn professional?

(Beat.)

JULIA
So it looks like I come in on page nine...

QUENTIN
We're not there yet, dammit!

JULIA
You watch your tone, Ducky.

GEORGE
My GOD! The ingratitude...

JULIA
I completely agree! I haven't even heard a single 'thank you' since I got here.

QUENTIN
Excuse me!

WERNER
Why is there yelling? Why don't we....

QUENTIN
Thank you?

DOLORES
Everyone just...

QUENTIN
THANK YOU?!

JULIA
You're welcome. See? Was that so hard?

(DOLORES reads from script, trying to get things on track.)

DOLORES
(As LILY) If only I had known...

QUENTIN
You're lucky to get any work at all at this point!

DOLORES
...that this road...

WERNER
Six times.

GEORGE
Shut your gob, Fritz!

JULIA
Oh! Is that a fact?

DOLORES
(To herself) That's not very good, is it?

WERNER
You call me 'Werner', or do not talk to me at all!

QUENTIN
It is the very definition of a fact!

DOLORES
(to herself) ...maybe if I were to use the subjunctive...

GEORGE
Toughen up, you Bavarian creampuff!

QUENTIN
Need I remind you...

JULIA
No! You needn't!

WERNER
What did you call me?

QUENTIN
...of your shining performance as Kate in Taming of the Shrew?

GEORGE
I'm sorry. "You whiney sausage-eater Werner."

JULIA
How dare you!

QUENTIN
What was it the critics said...

DOLORES
(to herself) ...had I known that the...

WERNER
Enough!

QUENTIN
"Even in the fifth row, I could smell the liquor
wafting off of Julia Crane."

WERNER
I cannot work with this oaf!

QUENTIN
"In the end, the Shrew won out...

GEORGE
Tough talk, sweinholt!

QUENTIN
"...at the expense of every ticket-holder in the
theatre."

JULIA
You memorized it. I'm touched.

WERNER
Why don't you hobble over here and say that into
my face?

DOLORES
Quiet, please! I'm trying to...

GEORGE
WHAT?!

QUENTIN
And still you think yourself worthy to judge my
genius!

GEORGE
Was that a crack about my leg?

JULIA
Oh! That's rich!

WERNER
Come over here, and I will crack it.

DOLORES
Werner!

JULIA
You sit here in your petty little kingdom, telling
yourself you're actually creating art!

GEORGE
Oh, that's it.

(GEORGE gets up too quickly, and falls.)

DOLORES
George!

JULIA
But somewhere deep inside, you know you're just
so much balloon juice!

QUENTIN
How dare you!

GEORGE
Stay there, Franz. Let me just...

JULIA
You surround yourself with these boobs, because
that's all you are!

(GEORGE manages to right himself.)

GEORGE
And I'm up!

JULIA
King Boob himself!

(WERNER starts to come at GEORGE. DOLORES stops him.)

WERNER
Ich töte Sie, verkrüppelte Esel!

QUENTIN
Get out! Get out of my rehearsal!

DOLORES
Now just hold on!

JULIA
Gladly! I leave you to your sinking ship!

GEORGE
This is for the fighting 35th!

(GEORGE lunges at WERNER. They struggle.)

DOLORES
Maude! MAUDE!

JULIA
And maybe one day you'll realize you don't have the talent God gave a cheap hairpiece!

(QUENTIN grabs JULIA by the shoulders.)

QUENTIN
Leave my hair out of this!

DOLORES
MAUDE! HELP!

(The door swings open. MAUDE enters, shocked and terrified.)

DOLORES
Maude?

MAUDE
Oh...oh god...

(The fights stop as everyone notices the visibly-shaken MAUDE.)

WERNER
Mrs. Myrtles? What is it?

(She looks at them, too scared to speak.)

QUENTIN
Maude, we're in the middle of something here.

JULIA
Quiet, Ducky. Something's wrong.

(JULIA goes to her.)

JULIA
What is it, dear?

MAUDE
I can't...oh my god...it's...it's horrible.

GEORGE
What's she blathering about?

MAUDE
I was just listening to... to Ramon Raquello. On the radio. Stardust, I think. And then... they said that...

DOLORES
What? What did they say?

(MAUDE looks at all of them, unable to really form the

words. She goes offstage.)

QUENTIN
What the hell's gotten into her?

GEORGE
She's having her monthlies.

DOLORES
What if something's happened to Dominic?

(Beat. DOLORES looks at JULIA.)

DOLORES
Dominic is her husband.

JULIA
I know who he is.

(MAUDE enters. She rolls in the radio with her.)

MAUDE
There was music... and then they interrupted the music.... a reporter... first, it was at Princeton.... they were talking to a professor... something happening in space... and then....

(She fiddles with the radio, trying to get the station back.)

MAUDE
It crashed in New Jersey.

WERNER
What crashed?

MAUDE
They thought it was a meteor...but it wasn't.

DOLORES
What was it?

MAUDE
They said it was a cylinder. A huge metal cylinder
that fell from the sky.

GEORGE
My god. Have the Germans invaded?

MAUDE
No. Worse. Much worse.

QUENTIN
The cylinder...Where did it come from?

(MAUDE manages to get the radio station.)

MAUDE
From Mars.

(The Radio Interviewer, CARL PHILLIPS, is heard.)

CARL PHILLIPS
Ladies and gentlemen, this is the most terrifying
thing I've ever witnessed.

Wait a minute.

Someone crawling out of the hollow top. Someone...
or something...I can see, peering out of that black
hole two luminous discs...are they eyes? It might be
a face, might be almost...

Good heavens. Something wriggling out of the
shadows like a grey snake.

Now it's another one, and another one, and another
one. They look like tentacles to me, or...

I can see the thing's body now. It's large, large as a
bear. It glistens like wet leather.

But that face, it's...ladies and gentlemen, it's indescribable. I can hardly force myself to keep looking at it, it's so awful. It's eyes are black, and they gleam like a serpent's. The mouth is a kind of v-shape, with saliva dripping from its rimless lips that seem to quiver and pulsate. The monster, whatever it is, can hardly move. It seems weighed down by...uh... possibly gravity or something. The thing's rising up now, and the crowd falls back. They've seen plenty.

The most extraordinary experience, ladies and gentlemen. I can't find words...uh....I'll pull this microphone with me as I talk. I'll have to stop description until I can take a new position.

Hold on will you please. I'll be right back in a minute.

(Music plays. They all look to MAUDE, equally terrified.)

MAUDE
It's the Martians. They're here.

BLACKOUT

END OF ACT ONE

ACT II

(Lights up. The cast has gathered around the radio, mesmerized and terrified.)

ANNOUNCER
We now return you to Carl Phillips at Grover's Mill.

CARL PHILLIPS
Ladies and gentlemen... am I on...? Ladies and Gentlemen, ladies and gentlemen, here I am at the back of the stone wall that adjoins Mr. Willman's garden. From here, I get a sweep of the whole scene. I'll give you every detail as long as I can talk, and as long as I can see. More state police have arrived, they're drawing up a cordon in front of the pit. About 30 of them. No need to push the crowd back now, they're willing to keep their distance. The captain's conferring with someone... can't quite see who... ah yes, I believe it's Professor Pearson. Yes, it is. Now, now they've parted and the professor moves around one side, studying

the object, while the captain and two policemen advance with something in their hand. I can see it now. It's a white handkerchief tied to a pole. Flag of truce. If those creatures... know what that means...what anything means.

(A strange sound is heard in the background.)

CARL PHILLIPS
Wait a minute... something's happening...

A humped shape is rising out of the pit....I can make out a small beam of light against a mirror.

What's that?

A jet of flames springing from the mirror. It leaps right at the advancing men! It strikes them head on! Oh lord, they're turning into flames!

(Men are heard screaming over the radio.)

CARL PHILLIPS
Now the whole fields, followed by the woods... the fires!... there's gas heading everywhere... coming this way now, about 20 yards to my right...

(The broadcast is cut off. All wait in terror what seems like an eternity. Finally-)

ANNOUNCER
Ladies and gentlemen, due to circumstances beyond our control, we are unable to continue to broadcast from Grover's Mill. Evidently, there's some difficulty with our field transmission. However, we will return to that point at the earliest opportunity. In the meantime, we have a late bulletin from San Diego, California. Prof. Endelcoffer, speaking at the California Astronomical society, expressed the

opinion that the explosions on Mars are undoubt-
edly nothing more than severe volcanic disturbances on the surface of the planet.

GEORGE
Idiots.

ANNOUNCER
We continue now with our piano interlude.

*(The broadcast continues underneath the following
dialogue.)*

QUENTIN
Turn it off.

DOLORES
I want to hear this.

JULIA
He's right. Turn it off.

WERNER
People are dying out there!

JULIA
And what are we supposed to do about it?

MAUDE
Dominic...

QUENTIN
We're safe for now. I haven't heard anything about
New York yet. Just New Jersey.

MAUDE
New Jersey is practically next door!

GEORGE
Goddammit!

DOLORES
We're all going to die!

(The music stops.)

GEORGE
Wait, shhh.

ANNOUNCER
Ladies and gentlemen, I've just been handed a message that came in from Grover's Mill by telephone. Just one moment please.

At least 40 people, including 6 state troopers, lie dead in a field east of the village of Grover's Mill, their bodies burned & distorted beyond all possible recognition.

DOLORES
Oh my god...

WERNER
No...

ANNOUNCER
The next voice you hear will be that of Brigadier General Montgomery Smith, Commander of the State Militia at Trenton, New Jersey.

GENERAL
I have been requested by the Governor of New Jersey to place the counties of Mercer & Middlesex, as...as far West as Princeton and East to Jamesburg under Martial Law....

(QUENTIN turns off the radio. Most of the others react badly.)

MAUDE
Quentin!

QUENTIN
I'm sorry! Were you planning to make a trip to Middlesex tonight?

DOLORES
We need to know what's going on!

JULIA
Haven't you figured it out!? We're under attack. Those things have come down and...

GEORGE
They're conquering us.

(All look to GEORGE.)

GEORGE
That's what this is. A war. An invasion. And we don't stand a snowman's chance in Hell.

JULIA
Steady, George.

(GEORGE pulls a gun from his jacket. All jump. He grabs MAUDE, kissing her deeply. She is too stunned to respond.)

GEORGE
In another time, I could have loved you.

(He bolts for the door.)

QUENTIN
George?! Where are you going?

GEORGE
There are soldiers out there, dying for the cause. Probably. And they need my help. Good-bye, friends. Shed no tears for me. Tonight, I go to my destiny.

QUENTIN
You can't leave!

(GEORGE quickly pulls QUENTIN aside.)

GEORGE
Quiet, you're ruining my exit.

(Immediately to the others.)

GEORGE
And so, with head held high, I go...

QUENTIN
Stop! We need you here!

DOLORES
We do?

QUENTIN
Yes, you dolt! George has military experience.
(To GEORGE) Please, just stay the night. Help
us survive. Tomorrow, you can... I don't know...
re-enlist?

MAUDE
Dominic... I need to get to Dominic.

*(As they talk, MAUDE has crept to the door. She's about
to leave when-)*

JULIA
Maude! Where are you going?!

(GEORGE gets in the way.)

QUENTIN
You're not going out there.

MAUDE
The hell I'm not!

GEORGE
If you ever loved me, listen to me now. Those cylinder things could be here any minute.

DOLORES
Which is why we should be listening to the radio!

MAUDE
I want to be with my Dominic!

WERNER
Let her go!

DOLORES
We need to listen to the radio!

(DOLORES pushes past QUENTIN.)

QUENTIN
Hey!

(He staggers backwards, bumping into the radio. It crashes to the ground, loudly. They all stare at it for a moment.)

QUENTIN
Well. That was helpful.

WERNER
No! The radio-box!

DOLORES
Maybe it still...let me just...

(DOLORES rights it, tries to get a station. Nothing.)

JULIA
Turn the knobs. No, the other knobs.

DOLORES
I'm turning every damn knob this thing has! It's not working!

JULIA
It's not working because you broke it.

DOLORES
I didn't break it. He broke it!

(She points at QUENTIN.)

QUENTIN
I did what now?

DOLORES
You're the one who knocked it over.

QUENTIN
You're the one who pushed me into it!

GEORGE
Shut up! All of you!

(Beat. MAUDE makes another dash for the door.)

QUENTIN
George! Stop her!

(GEORGE grabs her by the arm, pulling her into a bear hug.)

MAUDE
Let me go!

GEORGE
There you are...shhh...shhhh....everything's going to be all right.

MAUDE
Take your hands off me.

GEORGE
Don't you worry, lamb. George is going to...

(MAUDE stomps on his foot. He drops her.)

GEORGE
Ow!

MAUDE
I'm coming, baby!

DOLORES
Oh my God, Oh my God...

(GEORGE tackles her. A struggle ensues. QUENTIN & JULIA end up in it, too.)

GEORGE
Ow! My corns!

MAUDE
I'm coming!

QUENTIN
Maude, stop!

JULIA
We need to stay together!

MAUDE
DOMINIC!

QUENTIN
Listen to her! She's right!

JULIA
I know I'm right!

QUENTIN
I'm agreeing with you! Shut up already!

WERNER
We need to think of something!

MAUDE
I WANT MY LOVEY-BEAR!!!

(GEORGE manages to pull free, then points the gun at the group.)

GEORGE
Now, why don't we all stop behaving like Frenchmen and calm down.

JULIA
George.

GEORGE
Julia.

JULIA
Please don't shoot us.

GEORGE
I have no intention of shooting you. I just needed to get your attention. Now. All of you. Sit down.

(He motions to the chairs w/ his gun. They all sit. MAUDE sits, but appears to be in shock. GEORGE paces the room, as though briefing the troops.)

GEORGE
All right. Those things are in Mercer County. That means they could be here any minute. Agreed?

(They all ad-lib agreements.)

GEORGE
Good. Now, from what we've heard, I think it's safe to say they have us at a serious tactical disadvantage. That heat-ray is a nasty piece of business.

DOLORES
And if those machines could survive space travel and entry into our atmosphere, we can assume

that whatever they're made out of is incredibly durable.

(They all stare at DOLORES, again surprised at her insight.)

GEORGE
So what do we know? Definitively?

QUENTIN
These things aren't from Earth.

JULIA
Obviously, they're from Mars.

QUENTIN
George asked what we know definitively. And we don't know that definitively, do we?

JULIA
They were just talking about disturbances on Mars!

QUENTIN
That's not definitive!

JULIA
Oh for fuck's...Do you want me to go out there and ask them?

GEORGE
We can't take them on. Do we all agree on that at least?

(Again, ad-libbed agreement.)

QUENTIN
So. What is it we can do?

(Beat.)

GEORGE
We can hide.

JULIA
Hide?

GEORGE
Hide.

JULIA
I'm sorry, but..hiding? That isn't a plan. That's what you do in the absence of a plan.

GEORGE
Wrong. Sometimes, hiding is the very best thing one can do. We stay here for the night. We become invisible. Let them pass right over us, and then...

WERNER
I want to call mama.

GEORGE
No phone calls, you fool! They could be listening. We can't do anything that will bring the slightest attention to us. That's step one.

QUENTIN
What's step two?

(JULIA raises her hand.)

QUENTIN
Julia?

JULIA
I move that we try to fix the radio.

DOLORES
Second.

QUENTIN
This isn't the goddamn Chamber of Commerce.
You don't have to nominate things.

WERNER
Second.

JULIA
Look, let's just try to fix this thing. It's our only
chance to find out what's going on out there.

GEORGE
Fair enough. Werner.

(Beat.)

WERNER
You... you called me Werner.

GEORGE
Can you fix it?

WERNER
Let me take a...can I get up now?

GEORGE
Yes.

WERNER
I will look.

(WERNER examines the broken radio.)

WERNER
There is torn wiring. I am maybe able to splice
it.

GEORGE
Then get to it.

WERNER
I should say, without proper tools, if I can get it

working, the signal will be...

(He makes the "so-so" sign with his hands.)

QUENTIN
Just do your best, lad.

WERNER
All right.

(WERNER sits down w/ the radio, and starts working.)

GEORGE
We should lock this place down. Nail boards over all the doors and windows.

QUENTIN
I'm not sure we have hammers. Or nails.

GEORGE
Then we barricade. Any large furniture... desks, bookshelves, cabinets... drag them to the doors and windows. Then we need to break up into teams of two.

JULIA
Oh dear god.

GEORGE
What?

JULIA
We're not going to...repopulate, are we?

GEORGE
Keep dreaming. No, we need to explore the building. Take anything we can find that might be of use.

DOLORES
Define useful.

GEORGE
Food. Kindling. Anything that might be used as a weapon.

QUENTIN
Go through all the desks, see if anyone has a gun hidden in a drawer somewhere.

DOLORES
I don't like guns.

GEORGE
Know what I don't like?! Bear-sized aliens bursting down the door and incinerating us!

JULIA
Stop scaring her, George.

GEORGE
She needs to be scared. For all we know, they can kill us from miles away, just with the power of their minds!

WERNER
AHH!

(Everyone jumps at WERNER's cry of pain. DOLORES screams a little.)

DOLORES
What happened?

WERNER
I cut my finger.

GEORGE
Back on track, people. The plan is, we break up into three teams of two, and explore the building. Once we've gotten everything we can use, we barricade ourselves into this room until we come

up with a long-term plan.

DOLORES
Why in here? There's a lovely view of the bridge
from Mr. Albertson's office.

(GEORGE rubs his eyes.)

GEORGE
Wiggles, I can't tell if you're truly dense, or just
putting me on.

DOLORES
Don't call me dense, you...

GEORGE
We're going to hole up in here because it has no
windows, and only one way in or out. If those things
try to force their way in here, we can pick them off
as the come through the door. Understand?

WERNER
Wait! Wait!

DOLORES
What is it?

WERNER
I think I...let me just...

*(He adjust the knobs on the radio. It sparks to life
just for a moment, though the sound is full of static.)*

WERNER
Got it!

ANNOUNCER
This is Newark, New Jersey. This is Newark, New
Jersey. Warning: Poisonous black smoke flowing
in from Jersey marshes. Reaching Ball Street. Gas

Masks useless. Earth population, move into open spaces. Automobiles use Routes 7, 23. 24. Avoid congested areas. Smoke now spreading over...

(Static overtakes the transmission.)

QUENTIN
No!

WERNER
Verdamt machine!!!

(WERNER whacks it. The signal cuts out entirely.)

DOLORES
Did...did he say poisonous smoke?

QUENTIN
That heat-ray wasn't enough. Now they're gassing us like damn cockroaches.

JULIA
This isn't an invasion. It's an extermination.

(MAUDE begins to laugh, born more out of hopelessness than humor. They all turn to her, waiting for her to speak.)

MAUDE
I mean... my god... this is it? This is how it ends? Gassed to death with you...you...people? Everything I did... everything I wanted to do... I was going to be a linguist... I was going to live with the Tatungalung people of Australia... learn their ways... marry their chieftain... discover the cure for measles from their native remedies... I would return to America a heroine... a heroine... not a secretary. This isn't what I wanted to be. Who would want this? To spend every day harangued and belittled by a washed-up fraud

with delusions of significance? My god, it's all so ridiculous, isn't it? Just utterly...

(She stops, as if in deep thought. Then she bolts out the door.)

QUENTIN
Maude!

GEORGE
Dammit, woman!

(GEORGE takes off after her. The others go to the door.)

QUENTIN
George! Get back here!

JULIA
Look at her go.

DOLORES
She could've been a sprinter.

JULIA
He will not catch up to her, not on that bad leg.

QUENTIN
I wouldn't count George Loomis out. That man is nothing if not persistent.

JULIA
If there are aliens out there, they're going to see those two tearing down the street. Then they'll interrogate them and then the four of us are as good as dead.

QUENTIN
Well, what do you suggest we do?

JULIA
Don't ask me. Our master strategist just went limp-

ing into the wild blue yonder.

QUENTIN
Stop cutting us down and do something useful!

JULIA
Useful? Oh, that's rich, coming from you.

WERNER
I...I will work on the radio.

JULIA
You may talk a big talk, Quentin Farlowe, but you are easily the most useless person I've ever met. I know it, these two know it...your mother certainly knew it.

QUENTIN
My mother was a saint!

JULIA
Then why didn't you marry her!?

QUENTIN
Maybe I should have!

(Long, awkward pause.)

DOLORES
Why don't I go look for guns?

WERNER
Me too.

QUENTIN
No! You sit there and fix that radio.

WERNER
I'm not sure it can be fixed.

(QUENTIN glares at WERNER.)

QUENTIN
Fix. It. Dolores, go find guns.

(She looks at WERNER, clearly wanting to stay with him.)

DOLORES
I...all right.

(DOLORES is about to exit. GEORGE walks back in, a look of shock and fear on his face.)

QUENTIN
George, did you...?

GEORGE
I lost her.

JULIA
Lost her? What do you mean "lost her?" Did she...?

GEORGE
She was like a damn jackrabbit. I was right on her the whole time, then...woosh.

DOLORES
I'm sure she'll be all right. Really. She knows this town better than anyone.

GEORGE
No...I don't think she'll be all right. Not at all.

(Beat.)

QUENTIN
Why do you say that?

GEORGE
As soon as I got to the front door...I turned to my left and...people. In the street. Panicking. Not many, but...

(QUENTIN smacks GEORGE.)

GEORGE
Ah! Dammit!

QUENTIN
Pull yourself together.

GEORGE
I am together!

JULIA
Maybe I should hit him.

GEORGE
No one's hitting...Just let me explain!

QUENTIN
Go on.

GEORGE
These people...they were running.

WERNER
From what?

GEORGE
Black smoke. All over the place.

JULIA
You mean...?

DOLORES
Black smoke? Poisonous black smoke?

GEORGE
They're here.

(Beat.)

DOLORES
Oh god! We're all going to die!

WERNER
No! I will protect!

JULIA
Maybe we should try to surrender!

GEORGE
The hell you say! I'll kill myself first!

QUENTIN
Everyone calm down.

DOLORES
Oh god! I don't want to die! I DON'T WANT TO DIE!

JULIA
Surely they won't kill all of us, right? Maybe they can be reasoned with.

GEORGE
Tell that to those poor bastards in New Jersey.

QUENTIN
Enough! This doesn't change anything. We still proceed as planned.

DOLORES
No, maybe Julia's right. Maybe we should...

GEORGE
We're not surrendering!

QUENTIN
No, we can still go ahead with the plan. Barricade ourselves in here, and wait for the threat to pass.

WERNER
But Mrs. Myrtles...?

GEORGE
She's gone! I know it's hard, but you have to let her go. She...would've wanted it that way.

WERNER
I'm sorry. I...

QUENTIN
So. We're splitting up into groups, right now. We scour the building for anything remotely useful. Then we meet back here in twenty minutes.

DOLORES
I just want to go home.

GEORGE
NO! We do as he says! There is poisonous fog out there, and I'm not letting any of you go out into it. Not even her.

(He points to JULIA.)

JULIA
How sweet.

QUENTIN
George?

GEORGE
Yes, sir.

QUENTIN
You and Dolores take this floor, and the basement.

DOLORES
Why do I have to go with George?

QUENTIN
It's George, or me.

DOLORES
Why can't I go with Julia?

QUENTIN
Because we're going in man-woman teams. Dolores,
you search all the desks, drawers... anything at all.
George, you start barricading.

GEORGE
Got it.

QUENTIN
Julia, you and I will take the top two floors. The
highest level is storage space, but there might be
something useful up there. I'll barricade while you
search.

JULIA
Or, we could barricade first, then search together.

QUENTIN
What do you know about barricading?

JULIA
Exactly as much as you know.

QUENTIN
Werner.

WERNER
Ja?

QUENTIN
You'll stay here. It's imperative that you get that
radio up and running.

WERNER
Try to find strippers.

GEORGE
Find what now?

WERNER
Strippers! For stripping wires.

GEORGE
Oh. I...yes, of course. Wait.

(GEORGE pulls out a pocket knife and tosses it to WERNER.)

GEORGE
This might help.

WERNER
Thank you.

GEORGE
If, in the course of our searches, the Martian's break the perimeter...

DOLORES
Oh god.

GEORGE
Do not try to engage them. We clearly don't stand a chance against them.

JULIA
Clearly.

QUENTIN
Just retreat back to this room as quickly as possible. George and I will protect you as best we can. Understood?

(They all nod in agreement.)

QUENTIN
All right. Twenty minutes.

(DOLORES, JULIA & GEORGE exit. QUENTIN turns to talk to WERNER.)

QUENTIN
All right, Werner. We're relying on you to...

JULIA
(*Offstage*) Are you coming or not?!

QUENTIN
Give me a minute, woman!

WERNER
I know what I need to do, Mr. Farlowe.

QUENTIN
Good man. We're counting on you.

(*He exits. WERNER is alone, working on the radio. He works for a while, testing periodically. Finally, he manages to get a signal.*)

WERNER
So. It is down to you. And to me.

RADIO VOICE
2X2L, calling Say-Q. 2X2L, calling Say-Q. 2X2L, calling Say-Q, New York. Isn't there anyone on the air? Isn't there anyone on the air? Isn't there anyone? 2X2L....

WERNER
I am here! I am...

(*WERNER realizes he's yelling at a radio. He lifts it up, trying to get a clearer signal. It cuts out entirely. He continues to try to get a signal, but fails. It doesn't work, getting him more and more frustrated. He sits down for a bit. The total silence begins to make him nervous.*)

WERNER
He...hello?

(No answer. He takes out the knife to defend himself.)

WERNER
Is anyone outside of here?

(The sound of crashing and breaking. WERNER tries to hide. GEORGE & DOLORES can be heard fighting.)

DOLORES
(offstage) Goddammit, George!

GEORGE
(offstage) What?!

DOLORES
(offstage) You nearly broke my neck!

GEORGE
(offstage) Oh please! I missed you by at least half a foot!

QUENTIN
(offstage) Stop yelling, you two!

GEORGE
(offstage) She's the one yelling!

JULIA
(offstage) You're going to bring the whole damn Martian... OH!

(The sound of JULIA falling down stairs. GEORGE laughs.)

DOLORES
(offstage) Are you all right?

JULIA
(offstage) That wasn't funny, George!

GEORGE
(offstage) From where I was standing, it was funny.

QUENTIN
(offstage) Get back to work! All of you! And be quiet.

(WERNER goes back to working on the radio. He still can't get a signal. Soon, GEORGE re-enters, laden with machine parts. WERNER jumps a bit.)

GEORGE
Sorry. Didn't mean to scare you.

WERNER
I was not scared.

GEORGE
Here you go.

(GEORGE dumps the parts in front of WERNER.)

WERNER
Vas ist das?

GEORGE
I found a few more radios, and gutted them for parts. Thought you could use them.

(Beat.)

WERNER
You found radios.

GEORGE
Yes.

WERNER
Then tore them apart?

GEORGE
Think nothing of it.

(GEORGE exits. WERNER works in silence for a bit longer, clearly getting nervous. He hears movement offstage. He starts to pace and panic. He overturns the table, then hides behind it. After a few seconds, DOLORES enters. WERNER leaps up with the knife drawn, yelling loudly.)

DOLORES
AH!

(She leaps back, almost running out of the room. WERNER calms down. DOLORES has a bowl of candy with her.)

DOLORES
What in god's name are you doing?!

WERNER
I thought you were a Martian.

DOLORES
Do I look like a Martian?

(Beat.)

WERNER
I do not know what a Martian looks like.

DOLORES
Bear-sized. Leathery. Tentacles.

WERNER
Yes. Of course. I apologize.

(She leans against a wall, relaxing. She begins to laugh. WERNER laughs as well.)

DOLORES
You scared the hell out of me.

WERNER
I think you do not have so much hell in you.

DOLORES
Well, if I did, I'd have less of it now.

WERNER
Where is George?

DOLORES
Probably making his way to the basement. I ditched him.

WERNER
Why?

DOLORES
Mostly because he's George.

WERNER
I understand.

DOLORES
Dammit, I need a smoke.

(WERNER takes a pack out of his pocket and gives it to her.)

DOLORES
Thank you.

WERNER
Of course.

(He lights her cigarette, then lights one for himself as well. They sit in tense silence for a bit. WERNER points to the bowl of candy.)

WERNER
What is that?

DOLORES
Oh. Maude's candy. For the trick-or-treaters. I thought we might need something to eat.

WERNER
Oh.

DOLORES
Of course, it didn't look like there'd be any trick-or-treaters tonight.

WERNER
You went outside?

DOLORES
Just looked out the window.

WERNER
Did you see anything? Anything bad?

DOLORES
I saw some smoke.

WERNER
Are you all right?

DOLORES
I just saw it, Werner. I didn't breathe it in.

WERNER
Still, it is Martian Smoke. We do not know what it can do.

DOLORES
I love you.

(Beat.)

DOLORES
I think there's a very good chance we're not going to make it through the night. And I wanted you to...

(WERNER grabs her and kisses her.)

DOLORES
Oh. My.

WERNER
I love you also. Since the day I saw you.

DOLORES
I know.

WERNER
You know?

DOLORES
Well, for a while. You get... nervous around me.

(WERNER takes their cigarettes and puts them out.)

WERNER
I am not so nervous now.

(They kiss again. WERNER breaks away.)

WERNER
Wait. I know what this is.

DOLORES
What?

WERNER
You are here, with me, because it is the end.

DOLORES
I'm not following.

WERNER
If Texas man was here, and I was here, you would
choose Texas man.

DOLORES
Oh my lord...

WERNER
Three months you have been here. You are always going to parties.

DOLORES
Do you really care about that? This might be our last night on earth.

WERNER
You think they might take us to Mars?

DOLORES
Ah… actually, I meant that they're going to kill us.

WERNER
I see.

DOLORES
So let's stop talking. All right?

WERNER
When you kiss me, do you think of kissing Texas man's face?

DOLORES
Werner! Maybe they do things differently where you come from, but what you're doing, right now, is killing the moment.

WERNER
I am only…

DOLORES
I love you. And I want to be with you. Isn't that enough?

WERNER
But I…

DOLORES
Let me put it this way. You can either make love to
me tonight, or wait for the Martians to turn you
into a flaming pile of...Werner.

(Beat.)

WERNER
I see your point.

(They kiss again, beginning to remove each other's clothing.)

DOLORES
Wait.

(She closes the door. She turns to go back to him, then stops.)

DOLORES
Werner, you're right...I haven't been entirely
honest with you.

(Beat.)

WERNER
You have been lying to me?

DOLORES
Yes.

WERNER
I knew it. I was a fool. Why would you want to be
with me?

DOLORES
Wait.

WERNER
You come from good family, good American
family. I live in a tiny place with my Mama. We

can barely afford it. We wait for my Papa to return from Munich.

DOLORES
Werner, you're not...

WERNER
I read stupid little space stories, I watch monster movies. My Mama yells at me, that my head is always in clouds. I could not give you a good life.

DOLORES
Werner. Stop talking.

(He stops talking. Pause.)

DOLORES
Those parties... they aren't what you think. The man I was meeting there... Chester Wolcott... he's a publisher with Astounding Science Fiction. We've been meeting at these parties so no one would suspect. My father would have a stroke if he knew what I was doing.

WERNER
You are together with a publisher?

DOLORES
Not exactly, no.

WERNER
Then why...?

DOLORES
Because...because I'm D.B. Pennyworth.

(Beat. He just stares at her.)

DOLORES
I'm D.B. Pennyworth.

WERNER
No you're not.

DOLORES
I am. I really am.

WERNER
D.B. Pennyworth is a man. He writes space stories for...

DOLORES
Astounding Science Fiction.

WERNER
I am confused.

DOLORES
How many female science fiction writers can you think of?

(WERNER just stares, unsure.)

WERNER
Is Isaac Asimov female?

DOLORES
No.

WERNER
Then none.

DOLORES
That's because we write under fake names. When people see a story by a woman, they think "romance" instead of "robots." That's what Chester says. So we have to be kind of... sneaky.

WERNER
But you and this Chester aren't...?

DOLORES
I think you're more his type than I am. If you get my meaning.

WERNER
I don't.

DOLORES
Never mind.

WERNER
So you are…?

DOLORES
Dolores Breckenridge Pennyworth

(She kisses him. He smiles at her.)

WERNER
I just kissed my favorite writer.

DOLORES
How does that feel?

WERNER
Very confusing.

DOLORES
I'd imagine.

WERNER
All this time… you knew I was reading your work… but said nothing?

DOLORES
I didn't want anyone to know. Kind of pointless now.

WERNER
You pretend to not be smart so people won't suspect.

DOLORES
You're very clever.

WERNER
Yes, well... I am not so...

DOLORES
And you're adorable when you can't take a compliment.

(He's about to respond, but just smiles.)

WERNER
My favorite story is The Spheres of Saturn, when... when...

(They stare at each other for a moment.)

WERNER
Why are we still talking?

DOLORES
I have no idea.

(They kiss, then move behind the table. Suddenly, QUENTIN and JULIA enter. QUENTIN's head is bleeding. JULIA has a handkerchief on his wound.)

JULIA
Stop squirming. You'll make it...

(WERNER and DOLORES jump up in states of partial-undress.)

QUENTIN
What's going on? I've got blood in my...

(He removes his handkerchief, staring at DOLORES & WERNER.)

QUENTIN
Oh for Christ's sake.

WERNER
We weren't...I mean...I just...she fell.

(They start putting their clothes back on.)

DOLORES
Are you all right?

QUENTIN
No!

JULIA
He got hit by one of Mr. Albertson's awards.

DOLORES
What?

JULIA
We were moving a bookcase in front of the window. This five pound sterling monstrosity came tumbling off the top, and brained him.

(DOLORES giggles a little. JULIA gets the bottle of alcohol.)

QUENTIN
Yes, yes. It's a goddamn riot Never mind that I'm about to bleed to death. Werner, please tell me you got the radio working before you two went horizontal.

WERNER
It was... no.

QUENTIN
Damn it all to hell! What did I tell you to do? Fix the goddamn radio! And Dolores! Why aren't you with George?

DOLORES
I wanted to be with Werner.

QUENTIN
This is... I just... For fuck's sake!!!

JULIA
Calm down.

QUENTIN
What is so hard about...

(JULIA dabs alcohol on QUENTIN's wound. He lets out a girlish cry. As the scene continues, WERNER attempts to work on the radio, with DOLORES' help, but they have difficulty keeping their hands off each other.)

QUENTIN
How bad is it?

JULIA
Not too bad.

QUENTIN
It's going to need stitches, isn't it?

JULIA
Don't be dramatic.

QUENTIN
I'll be whatever I want. I'm the one who had a fucking civic trophy lodged in his skull.

(JULIA can't help but laugh at the remark.)

QUENTIN
You think that's funny?

JULIA
I do, actually.

(QUENTIN chuckles at it himself.)

QUENTIN
You're not helping, you know?

JULIA
Forgive me. I'll call for a nurse.

QUENTIN
I mean... you're undermining my authority.

JULIA
Is that what I'm doing?

QUENTIN
It's what you've always done.

JULIA
You might be right about that. Which is shocking, considering how rarely you're right about anything.

QUENTIN
My god, do you ever get tired of castrating me?

JULIA
Well, you make it so easy.

QUENTIN
I used to think you just liked to make a show in front of others, but no. The fact is, you're just a heartless bag of bile.

(JULIA stops tending his wound. She looks down, thinking.)

JULIA
You might be right about that too.

(Finally, WERNER & DOLORES' fooling around gets to be too much.)

JULIA
Dolores!

DOLORES
What? I wasn't...

JULIA
Go find George.

DOLORES
But I...

JULIA
Werner, go help her find George.

DOLORES & WERNER
All right.

QUENTIN
Werner, fix the goddamn radio!

JULIA
Let them go help George. I'm sure they'll only need...what...ten minutes?

WERNER
Fifteen would be better.

JULIA
Fifteen minutes. The radio can wait till then.

QUENTIN
No! I'm giving the orders around here and...

(DOLORES & WERNER have exited.)

QUENTIN
They're gone, aren't they?

JULIA
So it would appear.

QUENTIN
You know they're not going to look for George.

JULIA
I had an inkling.

QUENTIN
Well at least someone gets to enjoy the end of the world.

(He notices JULIA is off in her own world.)

QUENTIN
What is it?

JULIA
The end of the world.

(Beat.)

JULIA
How do you fight the end of the world?

QUENTIN
I suppose we'll have to fight it together.

(He offers her his flask. She drinks. She looks at him, her expression unreadable.)

QUENTIN
I thought I knew all your faces. But this one's new to me.

JULIA
It's gratitude.

QUENTIN
Oh. Well. Isn't that something.

(He takes another drink, and passes the bottle back to her.)

QUENTIN
I'm glad you're here.

(She stares at him.)

QUENTIN
If this is the end...and I'm not saying that it is...
but if it is, I'm glad you're here.

JULIA
Are you going to get romantic on me, Ducky?

QUENTIN
I'm not all that drunk yet. So it's doubtful.

(The both laugh at that. QUENTIN goes to the radio.)

JULIA
Don't muck around with that. Just wait 'til Werner
gets back.

QUENTIN
That'll be fifteen minutes.

JULIA
Not very likely. At their age, they'll be done in a
flash.

QUENTIN
Were we ever that young?

JULIA
Speak for yourself, Ducky. I'm still that young.
Perhaps younger.

QUENTIN
Still, I'm glad for them. They've been mooning
over each other for months. There's something...
hopeful about it, don't you think?

(They smile, enjoying each other's presence. Suddenly, JULIA's mood turns.)

JULIA
Stop it.

QUENTIN
Stop what?

JULIA
Stop being charming. It's not going to work.

QUENTIN
You've lost me.

JULIA
I'm not sleeping with you.

QUENTIN
I wasn't aware I'd made the offer.

JULIA
Oh, don't be coy. I was Mrs. Farlowe for fifteen years. I know this side of you. You make glib jokes, you smile your sweet smile, and the next thing I know, I'm grabbing the headboard. Well, those days are done.

QUENTIN
Julia, I'm not...

JULIA
We come in, see the two children going at it, and we get ideas. But that's not...

QUENTIN
We get ideas?

JULIA
What?

QUENTIN
You said "We". "We get ideas."

JULIA
I most certainly did not.

QUENTIN
You most certainly did.

JULIA
If I did, it was a slip of the tongue.

QUENTIN
Oh? And just what ideas did your tongue get?

JULIA
Stop! I said no, and I meant it.

QUENTIN
I heard you. And I wasn't asking you to say yes. I was just trying to fix this goddamn radio.

JULIA
Of course. Yes, of course. I'm sorry. I just...

QUENTIN
What? You just what?

(Beat.)

JULIA
Do you wonder where we went wrong?

QUENTIN
Oh Jesus...

JULIA
It's a simple enough question.

QUENTIN
Why on earth do you want to talk about this?

JULIA
Because for all I know we'll be dead in the morning!

(Beat.)

QUENTIN
Of course I think about it. But it doesn't matter now.

JULIA
Of course it matters. It was our last fight, Quentin. And we never finished it.

QUENTIN
Funny. I thought the divorce papers were pretty damn final.

JULIA
God, you never listen.

QUENTIN
To what? To your constant criticism? Forgive me, lamb, but it got a bit monotonous.

JULIA
I'm monotonous? Me?

QUENTIN
Your stabs at my writing, at my acting...

JULIA
Quentin! The last two years of our marriage, you'd turned into this bitter, angry...thing. How was I supposed to stay supportive in that?

QUENTIN
I made it to Broadway. That's better than...

JULIA
Two performances, Quentin. The Stain Upon My

Soul ran two performances. The backers couldn't back out fast enough.

QUENTIN
They weren't ready for what I was trying to say.

JULIA
You didn't say anything! You just stood on stage washing a stained shirt. For two hours. And then you shouted "Mother!" at the top of your lungs. And then blackout.

QUENTIN
I was pushing the boundaries of the medium.

JULIA
You were so damn busy reinventing the wheel that you didn't even notice that it had stopped rolling.

QUENTIN
And that's just cause for fucking another man behind my back?!

(Beat.)

JULIA
I didn't want to sleep with Orson. I mean, I did, but it's not...

QUENTIN
Don't.

JULIA
I just...I wanted out. And I did it all wrong.

QUENTIN
Yes! You did! Of all the people in the world...

JULIA
I know, and I'm sorry.

QUENTIN
Was it his youth? Was that it? Were you trying out
the new model?

JULIA
He didn't look at me the way you looked at me.
That's what it was.

QUENTIN
I loved you.

JULIA
No. You worshiped me. And so you couldn't see
me for what I really was.

QUENTIN
You're the greatest actress of a generation!

JULIA
I'm not! I never was! You saw this woman, this
wreck of a woman, and made her into Mary
Magdalene. Orson saw me for what I was. A
woman. Not a goddess. A woman.

QUENTIN
The boy is a fool. He wouldn't know talent if it
had its mouth around his...

JULIA
I've always wondered if you hated him for sleeping with me, or because he had the gall to be your
better.

QUENTIN
What?!

JULIA
No need for histrionics, Ducky. You know it just
as well as I do. He's a genius. He's a genius, and
you're...

QUENTIN
Why are you doing this!?

JULIA
Because if you can't face the truth on your last day on Earth, then when?

QUENTIN
And what truth is that, Julia? I'm dying to hear your take on it.

JULIA
That being a good artist has become more important to you than being a good man. So you've become neither.

(He rises, looking as though he might strike her. He does not. He looks into her eyes for a long time. She touches his cheek.)

JULIA
God, I'm so sorry. I am. But it's the truth.

(His anger melts away, and he lowers his head, defeated. She holds him to her.)

JULIA
I've missed the way you smell.

(He chuckles a little.)

QUENTIN
What?

JULIA
You smell nice. Cologne and pipe smoke. I didn't realize I'd missed it 'til just now.

(He smiles at that. She smiles back. She leans in, kissing him gently. He takes her hand.)

QUENTIN
You know, when you walked through that door, when George told me to let you go rather than beg, I thought about it. I said "He's right. I can have Dolores read the other part. I don't need Julia." But I decided to beg anyway. Because I wanted to see you again.

JULIA
You don't have to say that.

QUENTIN
I know I don't have to. I want to, because it's the truth.

JULIA
Would you...I mean...if you want to, you...

QUENTIN
What?

JULIA
You know what.

(He stares at her, then smiles. He goes to her, stands behind her, putting his arms a around her waist. He then quacks in her ear a la Donald Duck. She laughs.)

JULIA
There's my sweet Ducky.

QUENTIN
At your service, ma'am, as always.

(They stay there, enjoying the moment.)

QUENTIN
Do you really think I've fallen so far?

JULIA
Well, if so, then I can't think of a better time to start over.

QUENTIN
As a good artist? Or as a good man?

JULIA
Try being a good man first. It's easier.

(The door flies open. WERNER and DOLORES enter, looking scared.)

JULIA
My god. Has it been fifteen minutes already?

(GEORGE enters behind them, gun drawn.)

QUENTIN
George, what are you...?

GEORGE
Who stands to benefit?

(Beat. DOLORES & WERNER stand with JULIA & QUENTIN.)

QUENTIN
What?

GEORGE
Who. Stands. To benefit? My old Sergeant taught me that. He'd been a policeman in.... I want to say Iowa... and he told me "George, if you want to solve a mystery, the first thing to ask yourself is 'Who stands to benefit?'"

DOLORES
He's gone crazy.

GEORGE
Shut the hell up!

(All fall silent.)

GEORGE
The last hour, something's been buzzing around in the back of my brain. "Why now?" "Why did the Martians decide to attack now?" Our allies are trying to fight back the German war machine yet again. America is ripe for the picking. And suddenly... Boom! Martians. Their timing was so perfect... so very, very perfect.

(He lights himself a cigarette.)

GEORGE
So I've been walking around out there, wondering where Dolores has run off to, and trying to figure out why this whole invasion seems so odd. And then, I hear this... thumping sound in the bathroom.

WERNER
It's not what...

GEORGE
I think "Oh god. The Martians have gotten in, and they've taken Dolores." Well, turns out I was half right. Someone was taking Dolores.

DOLORES
You're a pig.

GEORGE
And you're a floozy! And...I don't know why, but for some reason, seeing the two of them there, pantsless and vulnerable, it hits me. Who stands to benefit?

(Beat.)

JULIA
Who?

(GEORGE points his gun at WERNER.)

GEORGE
The Germans.

JULIA
What?

GEORGE
Don't you see? It's perfect! We already know the damn Krauts are hell-bent on taking over the planet. They proved that twenty years ago. But we pounded them back to the Stone Age. Their ambition might have survived, but they had no way to act on that ambition. Until... now, go with me, because it takes a little imagination...

QUENTIN
Just put the gun...

GEORGE
Let's suppose Hitler's scientists make contact with something...out there. Something like Martians. Communication is established. A dialogue, if you will. The Martians want to invade, but they don't know the planet. They don't know who to strike, or if the strike would even be successful. Then suddenly...

(GEORGE snaps his fingers. They all jump.)

GEORGE
...The Martians have someone on the inside. A country giving them the lay of the planet. A

country with a rather sizable grudge against...
anyone?

(QUENTIN is about to say something.)

GEORGE
Against the United States of America!

QUENTIN
George. I need you to listen to what you're saying.

GEORGE
Think about it, Quentin! How has Germany been
able to go from a smoking crater in Europe to an
industrial warmonger in the space of a few years?

WERNER
Please, just let me get the radio...

GEORGE
The Martians have been helping them. Giving
them technology, teaching them the art of alien
warfare. My god, it's all so obvious!

JULIA
It is?

GEORGE
This has probably been going on for years! Years,
I tell you! YEARS! The Market Crash... Martians!
I'd wager they have infiltrators everywhere!

DOLORES
What in god's name are you talking about?!

GEORGE
Don't you see? There's a pattern here! A conspiracy
set into motion years ago, to weaken their greatest
threat. I mean, have you heard about the Martians
invading anyone else? No!

DOLORES
Of course not! The radio's broken!

GEORGE
Right! And it's still broken! And who was supposed to be fixing it? The German!

(Beat. GEORGE looks at the table and equipment WERNER had been hiding behind.)

GEORGE
What the hell is all this?

WERNER
I built a little fort.

GEORGE
Someone set it back up.

(WERNER and QUENTIN go towards it. GEORGE points the gun at WERNER.)

GEORGE
Not you.

(JULIA and QUENTIN right the table.)

QUENTIN
So. George. What is it you...um...think we should do?

GEORGE
Oh, you leave that to me. Werner, why don't you have a seat?

(WERNER sits at the table. GEORGE walks behind him, trying to intimidate him.)

GEORGE
Out of respect for the 6 months we've been working together, I'm going to give you this one chance

to tell us everything you know about the German-Martian Alliance.

WERNER
I know nothing about the German-Martian...

GEORGE
I thought you'd say that.

(GEORGE grabs DELORES.)

DOLORES
Hey!

WERNER
Leave her alone!

QUENTIN
George!

GEORGE
I don't want to hurt her. I really don't. But I guess that's up to you.

WERNER
Please. Please. Don't do anything crazy. Or more crazy.

GEORGE
How long have you been living in this country?

WERNER
A year. Wait. Thirteen months.

GEORGE
Just you and your mother, yes?

WERNER
Yes.

GEORGE
And where is your father?

WERNER
In Munich.

GEORGE
And what does your father do in Munich?

WERNER
He makes shoes.

GEORGE
He makes....! Wait, I thought you said he was a corporal.

WERNER
I said he was a cobbler!

DOLORES
George, this is utter nonsense.

GEORGE
You're not off the hook either, Missy. You've been fraternizing!

DOLORES
That has nothing to do with anything!

GEORGE
Oh, doesn't it? What about your thing earlier? Something about their machines surviving space travel and what-not?

JULIA
I'm sure she just...

GEORGE
How did she know something like that? Methinks our dear Dolores has been playing us all for fools.

QUENTIN
I'm sure there's a perfectly reasonable explanation for that.

GEORGE
Like what?

(Beat.)

QUENTIN
Dolores, give him a perfectly reasonable explanation.

DOLORES
I...I'm a science fiction writer.

(GEORGE laughs.)

GEORGE
Of course! And Julia's the Virgin Queen!

JULIA
Excuse me?

DOLORES
It's true. I write under the name D.B....

WERNER
She pretends to not be smart so that no one will find out she is smart!

GEORGE
Please. That's just ridiculous.

DOLORES
Everything you've just said is ridiculous!

GEORGE
Spoken like a German-Martian Double Agent!

DOLORES
Let me go!

GEORGE
Quentin, you're with me, right?

QUENTIN
I'm sorry, George. But I'm...unconvinced.

GEORGE
Oh god. They've gotten to you, haven't they?

(He raises his gun towards QUENTIN.)

JULIA
Wait! Don't do anything stupid!

QUENTIN
All right, George. Let's say you're right.

GEORGE
I am right!

WERNER
He's not right!

QUENTIN
Let's say for a second that you are. What do you think we should do?

GEORGE
Hmm. Good question. Very good question.

(Beat.)

QUENTIN
Have you considered...?

GEORGE
Oh! I've got it! We send Werner out into the streets. If the Martians don't kill him, then he's obviously in league with them.

WERNER
WHAT?!

QUENTIN
Alright, alright. Now what if they do kill him?

GEORGE
Than I'm willing to concede that I might have
been mistaken.

DOLORES
You bastard!

WERNER
I am not going out there!

JULIA
The smoke will kill him!

GEORGE
Doubtful. I'm sure the Martians designed the stuff
so it wouldn't affect Germans.

QUENTIN
George, there's a problem with your plan.

GEORGE
There is?

DOLORES
Yes! It's completely insane!

QUENTIN
If we lose Werner, then no one can fix the radio.
And you agree we need to fix the radio, don't
you?

(GEORGE thinks on that.)

GEORGE
You're right.

QUENTIN
Good. So let's just...

GEORGE
Yes! Let's send out Dolores.

DOLORES
What?!

QUENTIN
No.

WERNER
No!

GEORGE
That way Werner can still fix the radio...To prove his loyalty....and if the worst should happen, we don't lose anyone of importance.

DOLORES
WHAT?!

(WERNER finally snaps. He lunges at GEORGE, knocking him to the ground. The two wrestle for a bit, as JULIA pulls DOLORES out of the line of fire. GEORGE finally manages to get WERNER on the ground. He levels his gun at him.)

QUENTIN
George! Stop!

GEORGE
He attacked me! What more proof do you...?

(Suddenly, a loud crash is heard outside. Everyone freezes.)

JULIA
What was...

(More crashing.)

GEORGE
Quentin, take a look. Carefully.

(QUENTIN quietly peeks outside, then shuts the

door behind him. He speaks in a whisper.)

QUENTIN
They're here.

DOLORES
What?

QUENTIN
One of them is pushing its way through the front door.

JULIA
Oh god no!

DOLORES
What do we...?

(GEORGE grabs WERNER, getting behind him and pointing the gun at his head.)

QUENTIN
George!

GEORGE
They're not taking me! You hear me! Call them off, Kraut!

WERNER
I can't! I am not...

DOLORES
Let him go!

GEORGE
You call them off now.

(More crashing outside.)

DOLORES
Please, George. Please! Don't hurt him. I'm

begging you.

GEORGE
I'm trying to save us all! Why can't you see that!?

WERNER
Let me go!

GEORGE
Now or never, boy. One...two...

(QUENTIN closes in, getting GEORGE's attention.)

QUENTIN
GEORGE!

(GEORGE doesn't shoot, but remains ready to do so.)

QUENTIN
Give me the gun.

GEORGE
You want to shoot him?

QUENTIN
No. I don't want him shot at all.

GEORGE
They're going to be here any second! That's why he attacked me!

QUENTIN
He attacked you because you were threatening the woman he loves.

WERNER
Yes.

QUENTIN
What more proof do you need that he's one of us?

GEORGE
They've gotten you all turned around, Quentin. But don't worry. I'm still on your side. I'll protect you.

QUENTIN
I don't need protection. I need you to give me the gun.

(GEORGE just stares at him, gun still pointed at WERNER.)

QUENTIN
You're a good man, George. You've just been pushed to the edge.

GEORGE
No, I...

QUENTIN
Give me the gun, and trust me. As your leader. As your friend.

(GEORGE still doesn't give in.)

QUENTIN
You're not a killer, George. You're a soldier. You fight other soldiers, not innocent civilians. Look at us. No one here means you any harm. We're all on the same side.

(GEORGE looks at everyone. The reality of what he was doing sinks in on him. He gives QUENTIN the gun.)

GEORGE
I'm so sorry. I just...

(WERNER leaps up and punches GEORGE. DOLORES runs to WERNER.)

WERNER
You never touch me again!

GEORGE
I deserved that.

(WERNER is about to go after him again. A crash right outside the door. Everyone freezes. They whisper to each other.)

JULIA
They're here.

GEORGE
We need to barricade. Quietly.

DOLORES
Oh my God, oh my God...

(They all begin building a barricade in front of the door. Once it's built, Dolores, Julia, George, and Werner try to hide in the closet.)

QUENTIN
Everyone. Hide. Spread out. Spread out of the closet. If it comes in here, I don't want to present a single target.

(They all go to different corners. DOLORES goes with WERNER, JULIA with QUENTIN. The sound of more crashing outside.)

GEORGE
Quentin?

QUENTIN
Yes?

GEORGE
Still have the gun?

QUENTIN
Yes.

GEORGE
Good. Don't shoot until you have a clear target.

(The sound of crashing grows closer. Soon, the door starts to slowly push open. QUENTIN slowly rises, taking aim at the door. MAUDE can be heard as she pushes the door open.)

MAUDE
Hello? Are you in here? Hello?

QUENTIN
Maude?

(She turns on the light. Everyone is visibly relieved. GEORGE embraces her.)

GEORGE
Oh thank god. I thought I'd never see your sweet face again.

MAUDE
George... please... your hands...

JULIA
Maude!

(JULIA embraces her as well.)

JULIA
How did you survive?

WERNER
Did the Martians see you come in?

MAUDE
Yes. About that.

QUENTIN
Quickly, get behind the barricade. They may still be out there.

MAUDE
Wait. Just listen.

(WERNER grabs a piece of debris & hands it to MAUDE.)

WERNER
If the Martians come, you can hit them with this until they...

MAUDE
There are no Martians.

(Beat.)

QUENTIN
What?

GEORGE
Did we beat them? Did the Army chase them off?

MAUDE
They didn't have to. There are no Martians. It was all a hoax.

(Beat.)

GEORGE
So the Martians convinced people that...

MAUDE
No. George. Listen carefully. There are. No. Martians.

DOLORES
You can't be serious.

MAUDE
I'm afraid so. I'm sorry I didn't get here sooner.
Honestly, I forgot you didn't have a working radio.
I just assumed you'd heard. And then Dominic
says "Maudy? Should you check on...."

QUENTIN
Maude.

MAUDE
Mr. Farlowe.

QUENTIN
I need you to explain just what the hell you're
talking about.

MAUDE
All right. Let me just...Oh! Did you get the
radio working?

WERNER
Almost.

MAUDE
Try to turn it on. And then tune in the CBS.

(They stare at her, uncertain.)

QUENTIN
Go ahead.

*(WERNER turns on the radio. He splices some wires
from the other radios, and it sparks to life. He tunes it
to CBS. MAUDE speaks as they wait for the signal.
GEORGE goes to help him.)*

WERNER
Do not touch me, crazy man.

GEORGE
All right. I just...I'm so sorry. And to you too, Dolores. I...

DOLORES
I'm not talking to you.

GEORGE
Fair enough.

MAUDE
When I got home, my neighbor Morrie told me all about it. Apparently, there was an announcement at the beginning of the broadcast that we'd missed. It explained...

GEORGE
Shhh! It's on!

(ORSON WELLES can be heard over the radio.)

ORSON WELLES
This is Orson Welles, ladies and gentlemen, out of character, to assure you that the War of the Worlds has no further significance than as the holiday offering it was intended to be. The Mercury Theatre's own radio version of dressing up in a sheet and jumping out of a bush and saying, "Boo."

QUENTIN
Orson fucking Welles.

ORSON WELLES
Starting now, we couldn't soap all your windows & steal all your garden gates by tomorrow night, so we did the best next thing. We annihilated the world before your very ears and utterly destroyed the CBS. You will be relieved, I hope, to learn

that we didn't mean it. And that both institutions are still open for business. So goodbye everybody, and remember please, for the next day or so, the terrible lesson you learned tonight: That grinning, glowing, globular invader of your living room is an inhabitant of the pumpkin patch, and if your doorbell rings & nobody's there, that was no Martian. It's Halloween.

(The radio music plays. QUENTIN shuts off the radio.)

MAUDE
So. There it is.

JULIA
Son of a bitch.

GEORGE
Is that even legal? Playing with people's fears like that?

DOLORES
I swear to god, I'll kill that man myself.

GEORGE
It doesn't seem legal, does it?

MAUDE
I'm so sorry I started this...

WERNER
He is a bad man. A wicked, bad, wicked, bad man.

MAUDE
If it makes you feel better, it sounds like lots of people were fooled. Not just us.

JULIA
But there was smoke! In the streets!

MAUDE
Turns out it was the Bowers boys. They set fire to that abandoned tenement down on Second.

DOLORES
So it wasn't Martian smoke?

MAUDE
No.

DOLORES
It was just...smoke smoke?

MAUDE
Yes.

GEORGE
That mean-spirited, pompous son of a...

(QUENTIN, who has been sitting quietly, begins to laugh. Quietly at first, but it grows in volume. They all just stare at him.)

QUENTIN
He's a goddamn genius.

GEORGE
What?

QUENTIN
My god, it's brilliant. To use his program like this... he didn't break the fourth wall. He blew it up!

DOLORES
He just terrorized thousands of people.

QUENTIN
And he'll get off scot free.

WERNER
How?

QUENTIN
He had disclaimers. He told everyone it was a joke. My god, the CBS is going to get more free publicity than it knows what to do with.

GEORGE
He's a bastard!

QUENTIN
The most brilliant bastard in America. He's just made himself a millionaire.

DOLORES
The public will never forgive him. And the police...

JULIA
Quentin's right. The CBS wouldn't have put this on if they didn't know what he was going to do. I'd wager they have a team of lawyers ready to jump at this.

GEORGE
So...what? He just made saps of the entire nation and walks away smelling like a rose?

QUENTIN
That would be my guess.

(QUENTIN begins to laugh again. JULIA & GEORGE join in.)

DOLORES
I don't know why you think this is so funny. We could've gotten killed.

WERNER
And we tore apart the offices.

QUENTIN
Dammit. I forgot about that.

JULIA
How bad can it be?

(She looks out the door.)

JULIA
Oh.

QUENTIN
You'd best get out of here. Right now. If anyone from the station were to come in…

DOLORES
Go home? We can't just go home!

QUENTIN
I'll have Maude get in touch with everyone tomorrow to reschedule our rehearsal.

WERNER
What about the mess in the…

QUENTIN
I'll take care of it. Now go on. All of you. You still have something of an evening left. Go enjoy it.

GEORGE
Quentin.

QUENTIN
What?

GEORGE
We might not even have jobs tomorrow.

QUENTIN
Are you serious? Welles just tripled the demand for radio theatre in a single broadcast. I think we'll be fine.

(They all just stare at him.)

QUENTIN
What do you want to do? Hmmm? Sit here and discuss how we were all victims of the greatest trick in Halloween history? How we were all played for saps by the goddamn Mercury Theatre of the Air? Or would you rather go home to your loved ones?

(They all just stare at him.)

QUENTIN
Go! Go, go, go!

(MAUDE, DOLORES & WERNER speak as they leave. JULIA also exits.)

MAUDE
Good night, Mr. Farlowe.

QUENTIN
Good night, Maude.

DOLORES
I've missed my party.

WERNER
If you would like, there is a movie playing down on Fourth. The Invisible Ray. It has Karloff and Lugosi.

DOLORES
Ooo!

(GEORGE remains.)

GEORGE
So I guess I'll just go then.

QUENTIN
Good night, George.

GEORGE
Again...very sorry about the whole...

QUENTIN
Water under the bridge.

GEORGE
No, Quentin. I need you to understand...

QUENTIN
George. Water under the bridge.

GEORGE
Really?

QUENTIN
Really.

GEORGE
Well...good night then.

QUENTIN
Night.

(GEORGE leaves. QUENTIN is alone for a bit. He sits and touches the wound on his head. It still stings. Suddenly, the door creaks open , and the jack-o-lantern appears, held by JULIA. She makes a silly, ghostly sound.)

JULIA
Ooooooooo!

QUENTIN
Very funny.

(JULIA enters, fully.)

JULIA
I found this on the front step.

QUENTIN
It's Maude's.

JULIA
I thought trick-or-treating happened tomorrow.

QUENTIN
It's a community program.

JULIA
Well. There's church folk for you.

(She hands it to him, then starts to go.)

QUENTIN
Julia?

JULIA
Yes?

QUENTIN
If I... that is... If I were to call on you tomorrow, would you answer?

(She smiles.)

JULIA
Why don't you call on me tomorrow and find out?

(She is about to leave, then looks back at him.)

JULIA
Oh hell. Why wait?

(They laugh, take each other's hands & kiss. Lights fade. Blackout.)

THE END

ABOUT THE PLAYWRIGHT

Joseph Zettelmaier is a Michigan-based playwright and four-time nominee for the Steinberg/American Theatre Critics Association Award for best new play, first in 2006 for *All Childish Things*, then in 2007 for *Language Lessons*, in 2010 for *It Came From Mars* and in 2012 for *Dead Man's Shoes*. Other plays include *Salvage, The Gravedigger, Northern Aggression, Dr. Seward's Dracula, All Childish Things, Invasive Species, Dead Man's Shoes, The Scullery Maid, Night Blooming and Ebenezer. Point of Origin* won Best Locally Created Script 2002 from the Ann Arbor News, and *The Stillness Between Breaths* also won Best New Play 2005 from the Oakland Press. *The Stillness Between Breaths* and *It Came From Mars* were selected to appear in the National New Play Network's Festival of New Plays. He also co-authored Flyover, USA: Voices From Men of the Midwest at the Williamston Theatre (Winner of the 2009 Thespie Award for Best New Script). He also adapted *Christmas Carol'd* for the Performance Network. *It Came From Mars* was a recipient of 2009's Edgerton Foundation New American Play Award, and won Best New Script 2010 from the Lansing State Journal. His play *Dead Man's Shoes* won the Edgerton Foundation New American Play Award in 2011. He is an Associate Artist at First Folio Shakespeare, an Artistic Ambassador to the National New Play Network, and an adjunct lecturer at Eastern Michigan University, where he teaches Dramatic Composition.

Plays From SORDELET INK

It Came From Mars
by Joseph Zettelmaier

Ebeneezer
by Joseph Zettelmaier

The Moonstone
by Robert Kauzlaric
based on the novel by Wilkie Collins

Eve of Ides
by David Blixt

Printed in the USA
CPSIA information can be obtained
at www.ICGtesting.com
LVHW010540310723
753885LV00003B/475